INDIAN
COOKERY

BayBooks
An imprint of HarperCollins*Publishers*

CONTENTS

A BAY BOOKS PUBLICATION
An imprint of HarperCollinsPublishers

First published by Bay Books as Best of Indian Cooking *in 1984.*
This revised edition published in Australia in 1992
Reprinted in 1993

Bay Books, of
CollinsAngus&Robertson Publishers Pty Limited
A division of HarperCollinsPublishers (Australia) Pty Limited
25 Ryde Road, Pymble NSW 2073, Australia

HarperCollinsPublishers (New Zealand) Limited
31 View Road, Glenfield, Auckland 10, New Zealand

HarperCollinsPublishers Limited
77– 85 Fulham Palace Road, London W6 8JB,
United Kingdom

Copyright © Bay Books 1992

National Library of Australia
Cataloguing-in-Publication data:

Berecry, Wendy.
   Indian cookery.

   Includes index.
   ISBN 1 86378 034 3.

   1. Cookery India. 2. Cookery (Curry). I. Title.
   (Series: Bay Books cookery collection)

641.5954

Cover and chapter opening photography by
Ashley Mackevicius, with styling by Wendy Berecry

Printed by Griffin Press Pty Ltd, Netley, South Australia

6 5 4 3 2
96 95 94 93

DISCOVER THE DELIGHTS OF
INDIAN COOKING

While we in the Western world are just discovering how to add spice to our food, the Indians have been perfecting this culinary art to a high level of complexity and sophistication for the last 4,000 years. For those of you who thought that "curry and rice" are all that the Indian population of 843 million eat, you are mistaken.

The diversity of geography, climate and religion in India has meant that a tantalising variety of regional specialties has developed. For instance, the cooler climate around Kashmir and the Himalayas in the north has contributed rich, creamy meat curries, wheat breads and pancakes, chillies and the tandoor oven to the Indian cuisine, retaining the Persian influence brought by the Mogul emperors. The warm and sultry southern areas down to the Malabar coast are renown for lighter curries, coconut-based dishes and vegetarian foods.

Religious beliefs have been of major significance in the development of the Indian cuisine. Around 78 percent of the population is Hindu, with the remaining 22 percent made up of Muslims, Christians, Sikhs, Buddhists, Jains and Jews. Many Hindus are completely vegetarian, resulting in a very sophisticated vegetarian cuisine. Also, many Indians are vegetarian simply because they can't afford meat, and have therefore had to create nutritious and tasty vegetarian meals with limited resources.

A curry consists of meat, poultry, seafood or vegetables, together with any number of spices (more than 20 can be used in one recipe) and a liquid such as water, coconut milk, yoghurt, vinegar or cream to produce a "sauce".

While the list of spices and other ingredients in an Indian recipe can be long, the cooking method is generally very simple and quick, even for the novice. If the thought of grinding spices by hand is daunting, simply use the high quality ground spices now readily available in supermarkets, health food and Asian food stores.

The emphasis is placed on rice in an Indian meal with the meat dish being used as an accompaniment to vegetables, lentils, and bread, making for a healthy way of eating. Traditionally, all the dishes are placed in the centre of the table for individuals to serve themselves. Alternatively, each person is given a *thali* - a tray with a number of small cups in which is a portion of each dish, with rice and bread placed on the side.

One of the more unique and enjoyable aspects of an Indian meal is the emphasis on accompaniments. They may be spicy sambals with lots of chillies so individuals may add a little kick to a mild curry, or something cooling such as cucumber and yogurt to give relief from a fiery curry. Perhaps a tangy fruit chutney or vegetable pickle can be included, for a variety of flavour.

Desserts are not generally a significant part of an Indian meal, but favourites include fresh and dried fruits, coconut and almond-based jellies and custards, sweet rice, dumplings with syrup, ice creams and rose-flavoured desserts.

Serve an entire Indian meal or adapt a Western-style meal by serving, for example, a tossed salad with a curry, or perhaps curried vegetables with grilled meats or fish, or any combination you fancy.

With no special equipment or techniques required you can now enjoy a simple, fresh and healthy way to add a little spice to your life.

THE INDIAN KITCHEN

Due to the simplicity of Indian cooking, very little equipment is required. In fact, most kitchens will already have everything needed to create a delicious Indian spread.

Most cooking is done on top of the stove. Indians favour cast iron or earthenware cooking pans, however, saucepans and frying pans of any material are suitable. A round bottomed cast iron pan similar to a small wok, called a *kadhai* is most commonly used in India. Also, a cast iron griddle called a *tava* is used for cooking pancakes, flatbreads and kebabs.

For cooking most curries, lentils, rice, vegetable dishes and fried foods such as samosas and pappadams, a medium-sized saucepan with a tight fitting lid is all that is required. If it is non-stick, all the better. A wok is suitable for deep frying and for recipes that don't require a lid such as wet curries that need reduction.

If you don't have a griddle on your stove, a frying pan will do the job just as well or in the case of kebabs, a grill. All recipes state which is required.

If you prefer to buy whole spices rather than ground, you will need a spice grinder. Traditionally, a mortar and pestle is used for this purpose, and gives a very finely ground result. These days, however, most people prefer to use an electric spice grinder or blender. The blender can also be used to chop onions, nuts, herbs and other ingredients. A food processor can be used for these and other mixing and kneading jobs, but does not grind spices successfully so in this case you could buy spices already ground.

Rice is one of the key ingredients in Indian cooking and easy to cook properly. Cook rice in boiling water until tender, or cook by the traditional absorption method. Wash rice in a colander, place rice into a saucepan, a size that allows the rice to be at least 2 cm deep. Add enough cold water to come 2 cm above the level of the rice, no matter what the quantity of the rice. Bring to the boil, boil until water has been absorbed. Steam holes appear on the surface of the rice, do not stir. Place a tight fitting lid on the saucepan, reduce heat to very low, cook rice a further 10 minutes without lifting the lid or stirring. Test rice after this time. Grains should be plump, dry and slightly sticky, not wet or gluggy. Cook further if necessary.

Undoubtedly, one of India's greatest inventions is the tandoor oven from which comes delicious tandoori meats and breads now popular in restaurants. A tandoor oven is a clay receptacle, with rounded sides, standing about 1.6 metres high, with charcoal in the bottom as the heat source. It is obviously not a practical cooking medium to install in your home. In fact, even in the Punjab province in northern India, where tandoor ovens originally come from, they are more often found in restaurants than homes.

The tandoor oven relies on the intense heat inside, created by the hot coals, to cook the meat, seafood or chicken pieces very quickly. The food becomes crispy on the outside while remaining juicy inside. The food is first marinated either in dry spices or a spice and yoghurt mixture and is then threaded onto very long metal skewers and lowered into the oven. Naan, an Indian flatbread is also cooked in a tandoor oven by pressing the dough onto the inside walls.

It is impossible to create the exact flavour and texture of tandoori foods without a tandoor oven, however, a kettle barbecue comes close or you can use a very hot oven or grill.

You will find it easy to create a delicious, successful Indian meal with no special equipment or techniques.

GLOSSARY

Ingredients listed below form a good basic store of Indian spices and foods; the Indian terms are given in brackets.

BLACK PEPPER (KALI MIRCH) May be bought as small, black peppercorns and used whole or freshly ground, or as powder.

BAY LEAVES Dried leaves of the bay laurel tree, used in flavouring many foods. Substitute a small sprig of coriander leaves for 1 bay leaf. Note: substitution will alter flavour.

BESAN Flour made from chickpeas or lentils— low in gluten and high in protein. If not available, use the following substitute. Roast yellow split peas in a heavy saucepan, being careful to turn constantly so as to prevent burning. Cool, then grind in an electric mixer or food processor as finely as possible. Put through a fine sieve and then store in a tightly covered jar.

CARDAMOM (ILLAICHI) An important curry spice, strong and aromatic, available as pods and powder. Substitute 2 cardamom pods, crushed, for ¼ teaspoon of powder.

CHILLI (MIRCHI) Available as fresh, green chillies, dried red chillies, chilli powder, and chilli paste. Chilli gives colour, flavour and heat to most Indian-style dishes. Those who are not used to hot foods should use only a little chilli at first, and gradually increase the quantity as desired. Chilli can also be omitted entirely — the recipes will work quite well without it, though will not taste quite so exotic. Substitute 1 small capsium for 2 green chillies, or 2 tablespoons chilli paste for 2 tablespoons chilli powder.

CHILLI SAUCE A hot sauce useful as a dip for meat balls and other savouries; may be used in place of chilli paste in an emergency. Substitute tabasco sauce or tomato sauce as a dip. Note: flavours are different.

CINNAMON (DALCHINI) Available as bark (cinnamon stick) or powder; an important curry spice, aromatic, warm and sweet in taste. Substitute 15 mm of cinnamon stick, crushed, for ¼ teaspoon of cinnamon powder.

CLOVES (LAUNGI) Available whole or powdered; an important curry spice, strongly aromatic and pungent.

COCONUT CREAM (NARIAL) Concentrated coconut available in many supermarkets and shops specialising in Indian foodstuffs, often in the refrigerated section. Used as is or dissolved in water. Store in refrigerator. Substitute, for liquid coconut cream, an equal quantity of canned coconut milk or evaporated milk. Note: evaporated milk substitution will change the flavour of the dish.

COCONUT MILK Available in cans or may be made by dissolving coconut cream in water, 30 g to 60 g coconut cream to every ½ cup (125 ml) water, depending on thickness required. Substitute, for every ½ cup coconut milk, plain evaporated milk or ½ cup evaporated milk in which 30 g to 60 g desiccated coconut has been soaked and strained out. Note that substitutions will change the flavour of the dish. A useful blender method for making coconut milk is to add 250 g desiccated coconut to 600 ml warm water. Place ingredients into blender and blend to a smooth puree. Squeeze through muslin over a basin to remove the first milk. Repeat this process for second milk adding same amount of water again to the original coconut. This will freeze very well or can be kept in a refrigerator. The rich cream will rise to the top of the milk and can be spooned off and used separately.

COCONUT Desiccated grated coconut is used in some curries and Indian desserts, for making coconut milk, some chutneys, and salads.

CORIANDER (DHANIA) Used extensively in seed and powder form — this gentle, fragrant spice is an important curry ingredient which rounds and balances the hotter spices. Coriander leaves are often used as a garnish in Indian cooking and as an ingredient in salads, chutneys and some curries. Coriander is easily grown in a pot. It is also known as Chinese parsley.

CUMIN (JHEERA) An important curry ingredient with a warm, aromatic taste. Available in powder form.

CURRY POWDER Blended curry spices. Mixture may be mild or hot according to recipe. Commercial curry powders do not give the flavour of a home-made curry mixture.

CURRY PASTE A paste made of blended curry spices, generally more expensive but giving superior results to the commercial curry powders.

FENUGREEK SEEDS Used whole or ground in curries. Strong aroma and slightly bitter taste. Use in small quantities.

GARAM MASALA A strongly perfumed mixture of several spices. These may be bought already mixed where spices are sold, or made at home by using either of the following recipes:

20 g cardamom seeds
20 g cinnamon stick
7 g black cumin seed
3 pinches mace
3 pinches nutmeg powder

Grind the first four ingredients together to make a smooth powder.

Add nutmeg. Mix and store in airtight jar.

125 g coriander seeds
30 g cinnamon
60 g peppercorns
½ teaspoon nutmeg powder
60 g cumin seeds
30 g cloves
60 g large cardamoms

Roast the coriander and cumin seeds separately. Peel the cardamoms. Grind all the spices and store in an airtight container.

GARLIC (LEBSUN) A pungent bulb which separates into cloves; it is peeled then crushed, pounded or chopped to add flavour to all types of food.

GINGER (ADRAK) The root of a tropical plant, available fresh, powdered and canned. Preserved, sugared ginger is used as a sweetmeat. Recipes in this book specify fresh ginger, which should be scraped before being pounded or shredded. Vary the amount of ginger used to suit your taste. Substitute ¼ teaspoon ginger powder for 1 thin slice of fresh ginger.

GHEE The clarified butter in which Indian food is traditionally cooked. Substitute, as a cooking medium, cooking oil, butter or margarine; in bread and dessert making, use butter or margarine.

LEMON GRASS A fragrant herb which may be bought in dried form or easily grown in the garden.

LIME JUICE Fresh juice of the lime — a member of the citrus family. Substitute for 1 tablespoon lime juice, 1 tablespoon vinegar mixed with 1 teaspoon sugar; or use equal quantity fresh lemon juice.

MINT A refreshing, tangy herb used in salads and chutneys, as a curry ingredient and as a garnish. Easy to grow in pot or garden; also available in dried form.

MUSTARD SEED (SARSON) Used whole or crushed in curries; has a strong, hot flavour and is generally used in small quanities.

NUTMEG (JAIPHAL) A pungent spice, available whole or in powder form.

ONION (PEEAZ) Sliced or chopped onion, fried golden brown, is used as the base for most curries. The frying caramelises the sugar in the onion and releases the delicious flavour and aroma. Onion rings, fried or raw, are commonly used as a garnish, and onion is also used extensively in salads.

PAPPADUMS Paper-thin lentil cakes which may be bought in packets at supermarkets and specialty stores. When fried in hot oil they swell, curl and double their size.

RICE (CHAWAL) Brown and white, served with curry or as a base for dishes such as pilaus and birianis. See Rice chapter for further information.

SEMOLINA (SUJEE) Grain, made from wheat, commonly used to make puddings and sweets.

SESAME OIL A fragrant oil obtained from the sesame seed. Use in very small quantities.

SOY SAUCE Made from soy beans, very extensively used in Chinese cooking as ingredient and condiment.

TAMARIND PULP From the pod of the tamarind tree, used in making tamarind water, a common curry ingredient. To make tamarind water, soak a piece of tamarind (about a tablespoon) in ½ cup (125 ml) hot water and allow to stand for 15 minutes. Strain water into another container, squeezing tamarind pulp as dry as possible. Discard pulp. Use more tamarind pulp if a stronger taste is required. Substitute for ½ cup (125 ml) tamarind water, 1½ tablespoons tamarind paste or 2 tablespoons lime or lemon juice; or use ½ cup (125 ml) vinegar.

TAMARIND PASTE (IMLI) A convenient method of adding tamarind to curry, used alone or mixed with water to make tamarind water. Substitute for 1 tablespoon tamarind paste: 6 tablespoons tamarind water; or 1½ tablespoons lime or lemon juice; or 3 tablespoons vinegar. If a stronger, sour taste is required then more tamarind can be used.

TURMERIC (HALDI) A golden-yellow fragrant spice extensively used to colour and flavour curries, vegetables, rice and savouries. Saffron is an adequate substitute.

YOGHURT (DAHI) Milk curd, used in its natural form both as a curry ingredient and a curry accompaniment — plain, spiced or with cucumber, or other fruits and vegetables.

CURRIES

In this section you will find a wide range of curries to choose from, including beef, lamb, pork, chicken, duck, fish and prawns. And these can vary from koftas to kormas to vindaloos.

The curries range from mild to hot and it is entirely up to you to adjust them to your taste. The recipes here are rated as mild, medium or hot, but you can change this by increasing or decreasing the quantities of spices. Of course for a very hot curry, add lots of fresh chillies! If it's too hot, a little yoghurt or lemon juice will help to subdue it.

Curries should always be served with rice, and some Indian bread such as chapatis or naan. If the curry is very hot, it is wise to have a cooling accompaniment, often yoghurt-based. Or include some sambals to spice up a mild curry.

Curries are easy and quick to make as long as you have stocked up your kitchen with the many spices which are required.

Southern Curried Chicken

MILD LAMB CURRY

Mild

1¼ kg boned shoulder or leg lamb

¾ cup (90 g) plain flour

100 g butter

2 green apples, peeled, cored, quartered and sliced

2 onions, chopped

1 tomato, quartered

2 cloves garlic, crushed

2 tablespoons curry powder

1¾ cups (430 ml) stock

2 tablespoons grated lemon rind

1 tablespoon fresh lemon juice

1 teaspoon brown sugar

2 tablespoons desiccated coconut

2 tablespoons sultanas

1 tablespoon flaked almonds

1 Trim lamb of excess fat, cut meat into cubes, toss in flour, shake off any excess.

2 Melt butter in a frying pan, add meat, brown on all sides. Remove meat and set aside.

Mild Lamb Curry

3 Add apples to pan with onions, tomato, garlic and curry powder. Sauté 3 minutes then pour off any excess fat.

4 Add stock. Return meat to pan with lemon rind and juice, sugar, coconut and sultanas. Bring to the boil, reduce heat to low, cover, simmer 2 hours, or until meat is tender. Stir in almonds.

SERVES 4 TO 6

KEEMA CURRY

Mild

4 tablespoons oil

2 large onions, finely chopped

1 clove garlic, finely chopped

2 teaspoons grated, fresh ginger

2 potatoes, cut into 1 cm cubes

¼ cup (60 ml) water

750 g minced beef or lamb or pork

¼ teaspoon each: ground cinnamon, ground cloves, ground cardamom, ground turmeric

2 tablespoons ground coriander

½ teaspoon chilli powder

½ teaspoon ground aniseed

½ teaspoon ground cumin

½ cup shelled peas

4 tablespoons coconut cream

1 tomato, chopped or 1 teaspoon tomato paste (optional)

1 Heat oil in a large saucepan. Sauté onions until golden brown. Add garlic and ginger, sauté for 2 minutes.

2 Add potatoes and water. Simmer, covered, for about 10 minutes, stirring occasionally.

3 Add minced meat, cinnamon, cloves, cardamom, turmeric, coriander, chilli powder, aniseed and cumin. Stir over heat until water has evaporated.

4 Add peas and coconut cream. Cook until peas are cooked and curry is dry, stirring constantly.

(Add chopped tomato or tomato paste with the peas and coconut, if desired).

SERVES 4 TO 6

LAMB KOFTA CURRY

Medium

1 kg minced lamb

1 onion, finely chopped

3 cloves garlic, crushed

2 eggs

2 tablespoons oil

1 onion, thinly sliced

2 tomatoes, peeled and roughly chopped

2 teaspoons grated fresh ginger

1 teaspoon ground turmeric

1 teaspoon ground cumin

2 teaspoons ground coriander

¼ teaspoon ground cinnamon

½ teaspoon freshly ground black pepper

2 teaspoons chilli powder, or to taste

2 tablespoons white vinegar

2 cups (500 ml) water

3 tablespoons plain yoghurt

¾ cup (180 ml) coconut milk

½ cup shelled peas

1 Combine lamb, chopped onion, garlic and eggs and roll into walnut-sized balls or 'koftas'.

2 Heat oil in a frying pan, sauté sliced onion until tender. Add tomatoes and ginger, sauté until liquid evaporates.

3 Add turmeric, cumin, coriander, cinnamon, pepper and chilli. Sauté.

4 Add vinegar and water, bring to the boil. Gently drop the koftas into the curry, cover and simmer 20 minutes without stirring.

5 Stir in yoghurt, coconut milk and peas. Simmer for a further 10 minutes.

SERVES 6 TO 8

HOT BEEF CHILLI CURRY

Hot

1 lump of tamarind pulp, the size of a walnut

60 g ghee

2 medium onions, sliced

2 cloves garlic, crushed

2 or 3 green chillies, chopped and seeds removed

1 teaspoon ground cumin

1 teaspoon ground turmeric

2 teaspoons chilli powder

1 teaspoon ground ginger

500 g lean meat, cut into 2 cm cubes

⅔ cup (150 ml) warm water

1 Soak the tamarind in 2 tablespoons water.

2 Heat the ghee and sauté the onions and garlic until lightly browned. Lower heat and add the green chillies, cumin, turmeric, chilli powder and ginger. Cover and cook for 5 minutes.

3 Add the meat, cover, cook for 10 minutes.

4 Add warm water and simmer 1 hour or until the meat is tender.

5 Squeeze the tamarind and strain the juice. Add this juice to the curry and cook a further 5 to 6 minutes or until the gravy is thick.

SERVES 4

❖ **TAMARIND TIPS**

Tamarind is available from Asian and specialty food stores, as a paste, dried pods or pulp. Make your own tamarind paste by soaking the pulp in hot water overnight, then pass through a strainer. Store in a glass jar in the fridge. You can substitute lemon juice for tamarind juice in any recipe.

In India, tamrind juice is very popular and refreshing. It is used medicinally in many Asian countries, to cleanse the digestive system.

KASHMIRI KOFTA CURRY

Medium

750 g lean minced beef

3 green chillies, finely chopped and seeds removed

3 tablespoons plain yoghurt

1 teaspoon ground ginger

½ teaspoon ground coriander

1 teaspoon chilli powder, or to taste

2 teaspoons garam masala

120 g ghee

1 teaspoon sugar

1 tablespoon milk powder

1 cup (250 ml) warm water

1 teaspoon black pepper

½ teaspoon ground cardamom

1 Combine minced beef in a bowl with chillies, 1 tablespoon yoghurt, ginger, coriander, chilli powder, 1 teaspoon garam masala and 30 g ghee. Mix thoroughly and shape into small meatballs (koftas).

2 Heat the rest of the ghee in a saucepan. Add the sugar, milk powder, remaining yoghurt and garam masala, stir over heat for 1 minute.

3 Add ½ cup (125 ml) warm water and the meat koftas. Simmer until the water has evaporated, turn the koftas and add another ½ cup (125 ml) of warm water. Simmer until water has evaporated. Sprinkle with pepper and the ground cardamom.

SERVES 4 TO 6

Choko Salad, (page 58), Kashmiri Kofta Curry and Spicy Cauliflower (page 52)

KORMA CURRY

Medium

120 g ghee

2 large onions, sliced

½ cup desiccated coconut

2 cloves garlic, chopped

1½ tablespoons poppy seeds

¼ teaspoon ground ginger

**4 green chillies, chopped and
seeds removed**

3 teaspoons ground coriander

¼ teaspoon ground cinnamon

¼ teaspoon ground cloves

¼ teaspoon ground cumin

**500 g lean lamb or beef, cut into
2½ cm cubes**

⅔ cup (150 ml) plain yoghurt

lemon juice to taste

¼ cup chopped, fresh coriander leaves

1 Heat the ghee and sauté the onions until they are a crisp, golden brown. Remove onions and set ghee aside.

2 Combine onions in a blender or food processor with coconut, garlic, poppy seeds, ginger, chilli, coriander, cinnamon, cloves and cumin, and blend until smooth.

3 Add spice mixture to the reserved ghee. Cook over low heat for 5 minutes.

4 Add meat and yoghurt. Bring to the boil, simmer over low heat for 1 hour or until meat is tender.

5 Remove from the heat, add the lemon juice and fresh coriander.

SERVES 4

❖ **CLOVES AND CINNAMON**

Both these spices lose their aroma and flavour very quickly when ground so must be stored in airtight jars.
If you want to buy whole spices and grind very small quantities, a hand pepper grinder is just the thing.

PORK VINDALOO

Hot

This dish, a southern Indian delicacy, is usually very hot and sour. No water should be used when cooking the vindaloo. For a milder effect use less chilli powder (1 teaspoon for mild, 2 teaspoons for medium).

3 large onions, sliced

5 cloves garlic, crushed

1 teaspoon ground cardamom

1 teaspoon ground cloves

**1 tablespoon cracked black
peppercorns**

3 teaspoons chilli powder, or to taste

1 teaspoon ground cinnamon

2 teaspoons ground cumin

2 teaspoons ground turmeric

2 teaspoons mustard powder

1 teaspoon ground ginger

3 tablespoons white vinegar

1 kg pork, cut into 3 cm cubes

4 tablespoons oil

1 Combine two sliced onions in a blender or food processor with garlic, cardamom, cloves, peppercorns, chilli, cinnamon, cumin, turmeric, mustard, ginger, and vinegar. Blend to a smooth paste.

2 Combine meat in a bowl with a quarter of the paste. Stand at least 4 hours, preferably overnight.

3 Heat oil in a saucepan and sauté remaining onion until tender and light brown.

4 Add the rest of the spice paste, stir over low heat for 3 minutes. Add the pork mixture, cover, simmer over low heat for about 1 hour or till the meat is tender.

SERVES 6 TO 8

PORK AND POTATO CURRY

Mild

4 tablespoons oil

½ teaspoon mustard seeds

1 large onion, finely chopped

2 teaspoons grated, fresh ginger

1 clove garlic, crushed

4 potatoes, cut into thick slices

2 tablespoons ground coriander

½ teaspoon chilli paste (optional)

½ teaspoon pepper

1 cup (250 ml) water

¼ teaspoon each: ground cloves, ground cardamom, ground cinnamon, ground turmeric, ground cumin

1 tablespoon tomato paste

750 g lean pork, cut into 2½ cm cubes

1 teaspoon white vinegar

1 Heat oil in a saucepan, sauté mustard seeds and onion until onion is golden brown.

2 Add ginger, garlic, potatoes, coriander, chilli paste, pepper, water, cloves, cardamom, cinnamon, turmeric and cumin. Mix well. Cover and boil until potatoes are half cooked.

3 Add tomato paste, pork and vinegar, mix well. Reduce heat to low. Simmer, covered, for 1 hour or until potatoes and pork are tender.

SERVES 4 TO 6

DRY CHICKEN CURRY

Mild

The pan must be continually watched, as the contents may stick. If this happens, add just sufficient water to prevent it

60 g ghee

2 onions, thinly sliced

2 cloves garlic, thinly sliced

2 tablespoons curry powder

1 tablespoon tomato paste

1½ kg chicken pieces

squeeze fresh lemon juice

1 tablespoon desiccated coconut

1 Melt ghee in a frying pan, sauté onions and garlic until onion is tender.

2 Add curry powder and tomato paste, sauté 3 minutes.

3 Add chicken pieces, mix well, cover, simmer for about 45 minutes or until chicken is tender.

4 Add lemon juice and coconut, which will absorb any excess gravy.

SERVES 4 TO 6

BOMBAY CHICKEN CURRY

Mild

2 kg chicken pieces

2 tablespoons olive oil

2 tablespoons white vinegar

1⅓ cups (125 g) desiccated coconut

4 cloves garlic, crushed

½ teaspoon ground cumin

½ teaspoon ground turmeric

1 teaspoon chilli powder

½ teaspoon ground black pepper

1 teaspoon grated, fresh ginger

10 curry leaves

1 tablespoon sugar

1 Place chicken pieces in a saucepan, cover with water and bring to boil. Reduce heat, cover, simmer for 30 minutes or until chicken is tender. Drain, reserving 1 cup (250 ml) of liquid.

2 Heat oil in a saucepan, add vinegar, coconut, garlic, cumin, turmeric, chilli, pepper, ginger and curry leaves. Sauté for 2 minutes.

3 Add the chicken pieces, reserved stock and sugar. Bring to boil, reduce heat to low, cover, simmer for 15 minutes.

SERVES 4 TO 6

CHICKEN VINDALOO

Hot

2 large onions

6 cloves garlic

1 teaspoon ground mustard

2 teaspoons ground turmeric

1 teaspoon ground ginger

1 cinnamon stick, crumbled

2 teaspoons chilli powder, or to taste

2 teaspoons ground cumin

6 cloves

2 tablespoons white vinegar

1 tablespoon brown sugar

90 g ghee

1½ kg chicken pieces

1 Roughly chop 1 onion, combine in a blender or food processor with garlic, mustard, turmeric, ginger, cinnamon, chilli, cumin, cloves, vinegar and sugar. Blend until smooth.

2 Combine chicken in a bowl with spice mixture. Marinate for at least 4 hours, preferably overnight.

3 Slice remaining onion. Melt ghee in a saucepan and sauté onion for 2 minutes.

4 Add chicken pieces. Reduce heat to low, cover, simmer fro 45 minutes or until chicken is tender, stirring occasionally.

SERVES 4 TO 6

CHICKEN CURRY WITH SLICED COCONUT

Mild

60 g ghee

1 onion, finely chopped

2 cloves garlic, crushed

½ teaspoon ground cardamom

¼ teaspoon ground cloves

1 cm cinnamon stick

1 tablespoon curry powder

1 tablespoon curry paste

1½ kg chicken pieces

½ fresh coconut, sliced and with the outer skin removed

250 g fresh tomatoes, peeled and chopped

1¼ cups (310 ml) water

squeeze fresh lemon juice

1 Melt ghee in a frying pan, sauté onion and garlic for 3 minutes.

2 Add cardamom, cloves, cinnamon, curry powder, curry paste. Sauté 3 minutes.

3 Add chicken pieces, sliced coconut, tomatoes, water and lemon juice. Cover, simmer 1 hour or until chicken is tender.

SERVES 4 TO 6

STEP-BY-STEP TECHNIQUES

SOUTHERN CURRIED CHICKEN

Hot

5 dried chillies

2 tablespoons poppy seeds

2 tablespoons coriander seeds

½ teaspoon cumin seeds

1 teaspoon ground turmeric

½ teaspoon ground ginger

6 cashew nuts

2 cups (185 g) desiccated coconut

2 cups (500 ml) hot water

90 g ghee

4 small onions, chopped

4 cloves garlic, crushed

6 chicken breast fillets, cut into 3 cm pieces

juice 1 lemon

1 Combine chillies, poppy seeds, coriander, cumin, turmeric, ginger, and cashew nuts in a blender or spice grinder. Blend to a smooth paste.

2 Combine coconut in a bowl with ⅔ cup (150 ml) hot water, stand for 3 minutes. Press coconut through sieve, reserve milk.

3 Pour 1⅓ cups (350 ml) hot water over the coconut, stand 10 minutes. Press through sieve, reserve milk.

4 Melt ghee in a frying pan, stir in onions, garlic, and spice paste, for 3 minutes. Add chicken, fry on all sides until brown. Remove chicken and set aside.

5 Pour the 1⅓ cups (350 ml) coconut milk into the pan, simmer sauce until reduced and thickened.

6 Return chicken to sauce. Add the ⅔ cup (150 ml) coconut milk and lemon juice. Simmer 10 minutes.

SERVES 4 TO 6

Cut chicken fillets into 3 cm pieces

Blend chillies, poppy seeds, coriander seeds, cumin, turmeric, ginger and cashews to a smooth paste

After pouring hot water over coconut, press through a sieve and reserve milk

Southern Curried Chicken

CHICKEN MALAI CURRY

Mild

30 g ghee

1 onion, chopped

2 cloves garlic, crushed

1½ kg chicken pieces

2½ cups (625 ml) thin coconut milk

2 tablespoons fresh lemon juice

CURRY MIXTURE

1 tablespoon ground coriander

1 teaspoon ground mustard

1 teaspoon ground cumin

1 teaspoon ground turmeric

½ teaspoon ground ginger

½ teaspoon chilli powder

1 Melt ghee in a frying pan. Sauté onion and garlic until onion is tender.

2 Combine all curry mixture ingredients.

3 Add curry mixture and chicken pieces to pan, fry for 5 minutes.

4 Add coconut milk and lemon juice. Simmer, uncovered, for about 45 minutes or until the sauce begins to thicken and the chicken is tender.

SERVES 4 TO 6

SRI LANKAN CHICKEN CURRY

Mild

30 g ghee

1 onion, chopped

2 cloves garlic, crushed

3 to 4 fresh green or red chillies, cut lengthways into thin strips and seeds removed

1 teaspoon ground turmeric

1 tablespoon ground coriander

1½ kg chicken pieces

2½ cups (625 ml) coconut milk

2 tablespoons coconut cream

2 tablespoons fresh lemon juice

1 Melt ghee in a frying pan, add onion, garlic, chillies, turmeric and coriander. Sauté for 2 minutes.

2 Add chicken pieces and coconut milk. Bring to boil, reduce heat to low, cover, simmer for about 45 minutes or until the chicken is tender.

3 Add coconut cream and lemon juice, simmer uncovered for 5 minutes.

SERVES 4 TO 6

MADRAS DUCK CURRY

Mild

60 g ghee

1 onion, thinly sliced

1 clove garlic, thinly sliced

2 or 3 chillies, halved lengthways and seeds removed

3 tablespoons curry powder

½ teaspoon cumin seeds

2 kg duck, cut into serving-sized pieces

1 cup (250 ml) water

squeeze fresh lemon juice

3 tablespoons coconut cream

1 Melt ghee in a frying pan, add onion, garlic and chillies, sauté until onion is tender. Add curry powder and cumin, sauté 2 minutes.

2 Add duck pieces, stir to coat. Add water, bring to boil. Reduce heat to low, cover, simmer for 1 hour or until duck is tender.

3 Add lemon juice and coconut cream.

SERVES 4 TO 6

❖ **CURRY PASTE**

Curry paste is made by blending prepared curry powder with some vinegar, crushed garlic and oil, cooked gently and then stored in an airtight jar. Make your own or buy it ready made in supermarkets and Asian stores

CURRIED DUCK

Medium

3 tablespoons coriander seeds

1 teaspoon cumin seeds

½ teaspoon fenugreek seeds

1 teaspoon poppy seeds

4 cloves garlic, crushed

2 cm piece fresh ginger, grated

1 teaspoon ground turmeric

1 teaspoon chilli powder

1 cup (90 g) desiccated coconut

2½ cups (625 ml) water

90 g ghee

1 large onion, sliced

2 kg duck, cut into serving-sized pieces

2 tablespoons fresh lemon juice

1 In a dry frying pan, roast the coriander, cumin, fenugreek and poppy seeds until lightly browned. Do not let them burn. Grind to a paste with garlic, ginger, turmeric and chilli.

2 Soak coconut in 1 cup (250 ml) water for 1 hour. Squeeze out milk, reserve.

3 Melt ghee in a frying pan, sauté onion until tender. Add spice paste, sauté over a low heat for 3 minutes.

4 Add duck pieces, cook for 3 minutes. Cover pan and cook a further 5 minutes over low heat. Add remaining 1½ cups (375 ml) water and simmer for about 45 minutes or until duck is tender.

5 Add reserved coconut milk and lemon juice.

SERVES 4

CURRIED PRAWNS IN THE SHELL

Medium

1 kg uncooked king prawns

½ cup (125 ml) oil

4 large onions, chopped

3 cloves garlic, crushed

2 to 3 fresh chillies, chopped and seeds removed

3 cm piece green ginger, chopped

2 teaspoons ground coriander

1 teaspoon ground cumin

½ teaspoon ground turmeric

50 g macadamia nuts, ground

4 cups (1 litre) water

1 tablespoon sugar

2 teaspoons fresh lemon juice

fried prawn crisps, to garnish

1 With a sharp knife, cut down the back of the prawns through the shell to the vein. Pull out and discard the vein, leaving shell intact.

2 Heat oil in a frying pan, sauté onion, garlic, chillies and ginger until onion is tender.

3 Add coriander, cumin, turmeric and nuts, sauté 2 minutes. Add water, bring to the boil, cook uncovered until mixture has reduced by half.

4 Add prawns, sugar and lemon juice. Simmer uncovered until prawns are tender. Garnish with prawn crisps.

SERVES 4

❖ **COCONUT MILK**

When you make coconut milk for a recipe, make extra and freeze the leftover quantity for later use.

Coconut milk can also be bought in supermarkets.

MADRAS PRAWN CURRY

Mild

20 g ghee

1 onion, finely chopped

2 cloves garlic, crushed

1 tablespoon curry powder

250 g fresh tomatoes, peeled and chopped

2 tablespoons fresh lemon juice

500 g cooked prawns

1 Peel prawns leaving tails intact, remove back vein.

2 Melt ghee in a frying pan, sauté onion and garlic until onion is tender. Add curry powder, sauté 2 minutes.

3 Add tomatoes and lemon juice. Cover, bring to the boil, reduce heat to low, simmer for 10 minutes or until tomatoes are pulpy.

4 Add prawns, continue cooking until prawns are heated through.

SERVES 4

PRAWN AND CUCUMBER CURRY

Medium

750 g uncooked king prawns

½ teaspoon chilli powder

1 tablespoon curry powder

pinch turmeric

thin slice fresh ginger, cut into strips

1 clove garlic, crushed

3 tablespoons oil

1 large onion, thinly sliced

1 cup (250 ml) coconut milk

1 cucumber, peeled, seeded, diced

2 fresh green chillies, halved and seeds removed

1 tablespoon white vinegar

1 Peel prawns leaving tails intact, remove back vein.

2 In a bowl, combine prawns, chilli powder, curry powder, turmeric, ginger and garlic. Stand for 5 minutes.

3 Heat oil in a frying pan, sauté onion until golden brown. Add prawns and sauté for 4 minutes.

4 Add coconut milk, cucumber, chillies and vinegar. Bring to boil, stir over heat for 2 minutes.

SERVES 4

Madras Prawn Curry

BOMBAY WHOLE FISH CURRY

Hot

60 g ghee

1 small onion, finely chopped

1 clove garlic, crushed

½ teaspoon grated fresh ginger

2 dried red chillies, cut lengthways and chopped, seeds removed

1 tablespoon ground coriander

1 teaspoon ground turmeric

1 teaspoon ground mustard

½ teaspoon chilli powder

1¼ cups (300 ml) coconut milk

2 tablespoons fresh lemon juice

1 kg whole fish

1 Melt ghee in a frying pan. Sauté onion, garlic, ginger, chillies, coriander, turmeric, mustard and chilli, for 3 minutes.

2 Add coconut milk and lemon juice. Bring to boil, reduce heat to low, simmer uncovered until thickened.

3 Add fish, cover, cook over low heat for 20 minutes or until fish is tender; turn fish once, stir sauce occasionally.

SERVES 4 TO 6

*Bombay Whole
Fish Curry*

FISH KOFTA CURRY

Mild

1 kg white fish fillets

3 medium onions

1 bay leaf

2 green chillies, chopped and seeds removed

¼ cup chopped coriander or parsley

1 egg

2 tablespoons fresh breadcrumbs

250 g ghee

1 clove garlic, chopped

1 teaspoon ground coriander

½ teaspoon ground cumin

1 teaspoon ground turmeric

1 teaspoon chilli powder

½ teaspoon ground ginger

250 g tomatoes, chopped

1¼ cups (310 ml) water

1 Combine fish in a frying pan with a little water, half a chopped onion and the bay leaf. Simmer until tender. Cool, remove fish, strain and reserve liquid.

2 Mash the fish fillets in a bowl, add green chillies, coriander, egg and breadcrumbs. Shape tablespoons of mixture into balls.

3 Melt half the ghee in a frying pan. Add fish kofta balls, fry over medium heat until cooked, drain.

4 Chop 1½ onions and combine in a blender or food processor with garlic, coriander, cumin, turmeric, chilli and ginger. Blend to a paste.

5 Slice remaining onion. Melt remaining ghee in a frying pan, sauté onion and spice paste until onion is tender.

6 Add tomatoes, cook covered until tomatoes are pulpy.

7 Add the reserved liquid from the fish and 1¼ cups (310 ml) water. Bring to the boil, add the fish balls and simmer uncovered for 10 minutes.

SERVES 4 TO 6

CURRIED FISH FILLETS

Mild

1 tablespoon ground coriander

1 teaspoon ground turmeric

1 teaspoon ground cumin

½ teaspoon ground ginger

½ teaspoon chilli powder

½ teaspoon ground fenugreek

1½ tablespoons white vinegar

2 tablespoons oil

2 small onions, chopped

3 cloves garlic, crushed

1 cup (250 ml) coconut milk

500 g fish fillets

1 Combine coriander, turmeric, cumin, ginger, chilli, fenugreek and vinegar to make a curry paste.

2 Heat oil in a frying pan, sauté onions and garlic for 3 minutes. Add curry paste, sauté 2 minutes.

3 Add coconut milk. Bring to the boil, reduce heat to low, cover and simmer 5 minutes.

4 Add fish fillets, simmer uncovered for 5 minutes or until fish is cooked, turn fish once during cooking. Shake the pan occasionally to prevent the fish sticking.

SERVES 4

❖ **GHEE**

Ghee is used in most Indian dishes. It is butter with the water and non-fat solids removed. To make it, cut butter into pieces and melt slowly without burning. Remove from the heat and allow to stand for a few minutes. Drain off the clear yellow liquid (ghee).

SPICY DISHES

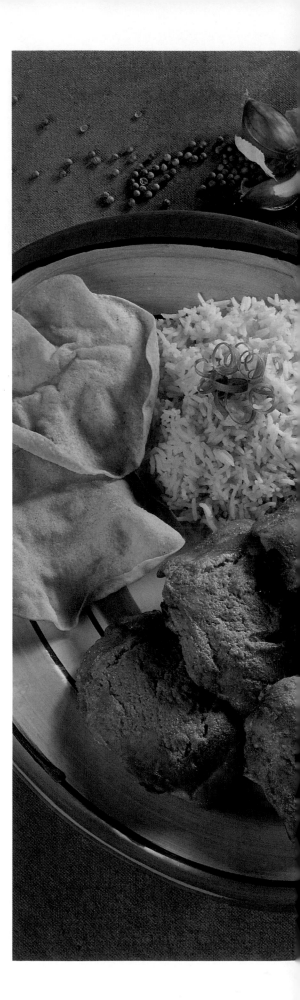

Try some of these tantalising dishes which combine a variety of spices to appeal to all kinds of taste. Serve these dishes with rice and accompaniments, perhaps a vegetable salad. Kebabs are best presented on a bed of rice, with some sauces, chutneys or sambals to complement them.

Ideally, spices should be freshly ground for optimum flavour, but they can be bought already ground from supermarkets. Often recipes call for whole seeds, such as mustard seeds or cumin seeds, which when dry roasted impart a rich aroma and flavour to the dish.

Or you may be required to grind a range of seeds together with some vinegar to make a paste. Make extra quantities of paste, and store in an airtight container in the fridge to use next time.

You can vary the quantities of spices in these dishes - be as creative as you want!

Tandoori Chicken and Spicy Kebabs

SPICED CHICKEN AND YOGHURT

Mild

60 g ghee

1 large onion, thinly sliced

3 cloves garlic, crushed

1 teaspoon ground ginger

1 kg chicken pieces

3½ cups (875 ml) hot water

1¾ cups (440 ml) plain yoghurt

½ cup chopped, fresh coriander leaves

¼ green capsicum (pepper), thinly sliced

½ teaspoon ground turmeric

1 teaspoon garam masala

1 Melt ghee in a frying pan, sauté onion until tender. Add garlic and ginger, sauté 2 minutes.

2 Add chicken pieces, brown on all sides.

3 Add hot water. Simmer, uncovered, for about 45 minutes or until chicken is tender and about 4 tablespoons gravy remain.

4 Add yoghurt, coriander, capsicum, turmeric and garam masala. Stir thoroughly, bring to the boil and remove from heat.

SERVES 4 TO 6

SPICY BAKED MARINATED CHICKEN

Mild

1½ kg chicken

2 medium onions, chopped

3 cloves garlic, chopped

¼ teaspoon ground cloves

½ teaspoon cracked pepper

½ teaspoon ground ginger

1 teaspoon chilli powder

2/3 cup (160 ml) plain yoghurt

1 tablespoon white vinegar

60 g butter, melted

1 Prick the chicken all over with a fork, truss with string.

2 Combine onions, garlic, cloves, pepper, ginger, chilli, yoghurt and vinegar in a blender or food processor. Blend to a paste.

3 Rub paste over chicken, marinate 1 to 2 hours.

4 Spread chicken on a rotary spit. Baste with butter, cook on moderate heat for 1 hour or until tender. If you do not have a spit, place chicken into a baking dish, baste with butter, bake in moderate oven for 1½ hours or until tender.

SERVES 4 TO 6

CHICKEN BIRIANI

Mild

4½ cups (750 g) rice

pinch saffron strands

½ cup (125 ml) water

125 g ghee

2 large onions, sliced

2 cloves garlic, crushed

4 green chillies, chopped and seeds removed

1 kg chicken pieces

1¼ cups (310 ml) plain yoghurt

1 teaspoon ground ginger

4 cardamom seeds

1 teaspoon black cumin seeds

4 cloves

1 stick cinnamon

few sprigs mint

1 Soak rice in cold water for 30 minutes, drain.

2 Soak the saffron in the ½ cup water.

3 Melt ghee in an oven proof dish. Sauté onions, garlic and chillies until onions are tender. Add chicken, yoghurt, ginger, cardamom, cumin, cloves and cinnamon. Cook for 15 minutes, stirring often.

4 Add mint sprigs, top with rice, saffron and water, cover, bring to the boil. Transfer to moderate oven for 45 minutes or until the rice is cooked.

SERVES 8 TO 10

SPICED GRILLED CHICKEN

Mild

2 kg chicken pieces

2 cloves garlic, crushed

½ teaspoon ground ginger

½ teaspoon chilli powder

1 teaspoon curry powder

½ teaspoon ground turmeric

30 g ghee, melted

1 Prick chicken pieces all over with a fork.

2 Combine garlic, ginger, chilli, curry powder and turmeric. Rub well into the chicken pieces, marinate for at least 2 hours.

3 Brush chicken all over with ghee. Cook under preheated grill on medium heat for 20 minutes or until chicken is tender, turn chicken occasionally.

SERVES 4 TO 6

MURGH MUSSALLAM

Medium

1½ kg chicken

4 cloves garlic, chopped

1 tablespoon poppy seeds

½ teaspoon cardamom seeds

½ teaspoon cumin seeds

2 teaspoons ground cumin

¼ teaspoon ground cloves

1 teaspoon ground ginger

1 teaspoon ground cinnamon

½ teaspoon cracked black pepper

1 teaspoon chilli powder

125 g ghee

3 large onions, thinly sliced

1¾ cups (430 ml) plain yoghurt

1 Truss the chicken.

2 Grind garlic, poppy seeds, cardamom, cumin seeds, ground cumin, cloves, ginger, cinnamon, pepper and chilli to a paste with a little water.

3 Rub the chicken with the paste.

4 Melt ghee in a large saucepan, sauté onions until brown. Remove onions and set aside.

5 Add chicken to saucepan, fry on all sides until lightly browned.

6 Return onion to the saucepan with yoghurt. Bring to boil, reduce heat to low, cover, simmer for 45 minutes or until chicken is tender.

7 Uncover pan, cook until liquid has evaporated.

SERVES 4 TO 6

COUNTRY CAPTAIN

Mild

Boiled, roasted or barbecue chicken is suitable for this recipe

1 large cooked chicken

60 g ghee

2 onions, chopped

1 clove garlic, sliced

2 green chillies, chopped and seeds removed

2 teaspoons grated, fresh ginger

½ teaspoon ground turmeric

1 cup (250 ml) chicken stock

1 Remove chicken meat from bones and break into bite-sized pieces.

2 Melt ghee in a frying pan, sauté onions and garlic until onion is tender.

3 Add chillies, ginger, turmeric and chicken, sauté for 3 minutes.

4 Add stock, bring to boil, reduce heat to low, simmer uncovered for 5 minutes.

SERVES 4 TO 6

❖ **GRATED GINGER**

Blend some pieces of fresh ginger with a little white vinegar and store in the fridge in an airtight jar. Use whenever fresh ginger is required in a recipe.

STEP-BY-STEP TECHNIQUES

Remove skin from chicken pieces, and make 3 to 4 cuts on each side

Combine onion, garlic, spices, yoghurt, vinegar, Worcestershire sauce and lemon juice in a blender, until smooth

Place chicken on a rack over a baking dish and bake until chicken is tender

Tandoori Chicken

TANDOORI CHICKEN

Mild

Tandoori chicken is traditionally cooked in a special kind of oven know as a 'tandoor'. Charcoal is put inside an earthenware oven and made red hot. The chicken or meat is put inside on skewers. The meats cooked in these ovens is superb; no other method gives you the same delicious flavour. Good results however can be achieved in your kitchen oven or on a rotary spit.

8 chicken thighs, skin removed

1 large onion, chopped

4 cloves garlic, chopped

½ teaspoon ground ginger

1 teaspoon ground coriander

½ teaspoon ground cumin

2 teaspoons ground turmeric

½ teaspoon chilli powder

½ cup (125 ml) plain yoghurt

1 tablespoon white vinegar

1 tablespoon Worcestershire sauce

4 tablespoons fresh lemon juice

1 teaspoon garam masala

1 Make 3 or 4 cuts on each side of the chicken pieces.

2 Combine onion, garlic, ginger, coriander, cumin, turmeric, chilli, yoghurt, vinegar, Worcestershire sauce and half the lemon juice in a blender or food processor. Blend until smooth.

3 Pour spice mixture over chicken, refrigerate at least 6 hours, preferably overnight.

4 Place chicken on a rack in a baking dish. Bake in moderately hot oven for 45 minutes or until chicken is tender.

5 Sprinkle with garam masala and remaining lemon juice to serve.

SERVES 4 TO 6

Mulligatawny Soup

MULLIGATAWNY SOUP

Medium

*Though called a soup, Mulligatawny is a meal in itself
and can be served as a main course.*

2 tablespoons ghee
1 onion, thinly sliced
1 tablespoon cracked black pepper
½ teaspoon ground ginger
2 teaspoons ground turmeric
1 tablespoon ground coriander
1 teaspoon chilli powder
1 kg chicken pieces
4 cups (1 litre) water

1 Melt ghee in a saucepan and sauté onion
until tender. Add pepper, ginger, turmeric,
coriander and chilli.

2 Add chicken pieces and water. Bring to
the boil, reduce heat to low, cover, simmer
for 45 minutes or until chicken is tender.

SERVES 4 TO 6

SPICY AND SOUR MEAT

Mild

3 cloves garlic, crushed

2 medium onions, finely chopped

½ teaspoon garam masala

¼ teaspoon ground ginger

½ teaspoon ground turmeric

2 teaspoons ground cumin

3 tablespoons white vinegar

30 g ghee

500 g lean beef, cut into 2½ cm cubes

1 cup (250 ml) water

1 Combine garlic, onions, garam masala, ginger, turmeric, cumin and 2 tablespoons vinegar.

2 Heat the ghee and fry the spice mixture for 5 minutes, stirring occasionally.

3 Add beef, fry until brown, stirring constantly to prevent burning.

4 Add remaining vinegar and water. Cover, simmer on very low heat for about 1 hour or until meat is tender. Stir occasionally to prevent sticking and burning.

SERVES 4

SPICY LAMB CUTLETS

Mild

500 g lamb, minced

1 large potato, boiled and mashed

4 cloves garlic, crushed

1 large onion, chopped

1 green capsicum (pepper), chopped

1 tablespoon chopped parsley

½ teaspoon ground turmeric

½ teaspoon ground ginger

1 teaspoon ground cumin

4 eggs

dried breadcrumbs

4 tablespoons oil

1 Combine mince, potato, garlic, onion, capsicum, parsley, turmeric, ginger, cumin, and 1 egg in a bowl.

2 Beat together remaining 3 eggs.

3 Take a portion of mixture and shape into a cutlet, repeat with remaining mixture.

4 Dip cutlets in beaten egg and coat with breadcrumbs.

5 Heat oil and fry the cutlets on medium heat for about 5 minutes each side or until meat is cooked and brown on both sides. Drain and serve.

SERVES 4

SPICY BARBECUED KEBABS

Mild

Kebabs can be made from minced or cubed meat and are either barbecued or grilled. Essentially dry, they are best served with salads and parathas.

1 teaspoon poppy seeds

1 teaspoon ground ginger

2 teaspoons ground coriander

1 teaspoon ground turmeric

¼ teaspoon chilli powder

1 teaspoon onion juice

1 tablespoon plain yoghurt

500 g lamb, beef or pork, cut in 2½ cm cubes

30 g ghee

1 Mix all the spices including the onion juice. Add the yoghurt.

2 Mix the meat well with the yoghurt and spices. Stand at least 30 minutes, preferably overnight.

3 Thread on skewers, cook on a barbecue or under a preheated grill. Turn once and baste occasionally with melted ghee during cooking.

SERVES 4

❖ **ONION JUICE**

Onion juice is extracted by chopping an onion, putting it in a mortar with 2 teaspoons cold water and pounding carefully. Then squeeze the whole through a piece of muslin or very fine sieve.

Fish Kebabs

FISH KEBABS

Medium

1 onion, chopped

⅔ cup (160 ml) plain yoghurt

2 cloves garlic, chopped

½ teaspoon ground ginger

1 teaspoon chilli powder

2 teaspoons garam masala

**1 kg firm-fleshed fish fillets,
cut in 2 cm cubes**

melted butter for basting

1 Combine onion in a blender or food
processor with yoghurt, garlic, ginger, chilli
and garam masala. Blend until smooth.

2 Combine fish with this mixture. Marinate
for 2 hours. Drain and dry.

3 Thread fish cubes onto skewers. Cook
under preheated grill for 3 minutes on each
side or until cooked through, brush with
melted butter while grilling.

SERVES 4 TO 6

SEEKH KEBABS

Mild

500 g very finely ground minced beef

1 egg

1 teaspoon ground coriander

½ teaspoon ground cumin

¼ teaspoon chilli powder

½ teaspoon garam masala

45 g ghee, melted

1 lemon, sliced

1 onion, sliced

1 tomato, sliced

1 Combine mince in a bowl with egg,
coriander, cumin, chilli and garam masala.

2 Apply some oil to fingers and skewer.
Mould heaped tablespoons of meat in a long
cigar shape on the skewers.

3 Brush with ghee, cook gently under
preheated grill until browned, turn skewers
occasionally.

4 When kebabs are ready, slide them off
skewers. Serve with slices of lemon, onion
and tomato arranged around them.

SERVES 4 TO 6

STEAMED WHOLE FISH

Mild

1 x 500 g whole white fish

15 g toasted almonds

2 bay leaves

½ green capsicum (pepper), sliced

1 tablespoon oil

1¼ cups (310 ml) plain yoghurt

½ teaspoon garam masala

½ teaspoon sugar

1 Clean and score the fish, place into a
steamer.

2 Combine almonds, bay leaves, capsicum,
oil, yoghurt, garam masala and sugar, spoon
over fish.

3 Place steamer over a saucepan of
simmering water, cook for 20 minutes or
until fish is tender.

SERVES 2 TO 4

❖ **STORING CUMIN**

*Once it has been ground,
cumin loses its flavour
and aroma very quickly.
Store ground cumin in
an airtight jar in a
cool, dark place to
preserve it. Use freshly
ground cumin whenever
possible.*

FISH MOLEE

Mild

A molee is essentially a Southern Indian, Sri Lankan or Malay dish, the basis of which is coconut milk. Vegetables, fish or meat can be used.

60 g ghee

1 onion, chopped

1 clove garlic, crushed

2 teaspoons grated, fresh ginger

1 teaspoon ground turmeric

4 green chillies, finely chopped and seeds removed

1 cup (250 ml) coconut cream

600g fish fillets

1 Heat ghee in a frying pan, sauté onion, garlic and ginger until onion is tender.

2 Add turmeric and green chillies, sauté 1 minute.

3 Add coconut cream. Bring to boil, cover, reduce heat to low, simmer for 3 minutes.

4 Add fish fillets. Cook uncovered for 4 minutes or until fish is tender, turn fish once during cooking.

SERVES 4

❖ **BEWARE OF CHILLIES**

Make sure you wash your hands throroughly after chopping chillies as they can irritate the skin, and can cause a lot of pain if you touch your eyes.

SPICY BAKED FISH FILLETS

Mild

500 g white fish fillets

4 red chillies, finely chopped and seeds removed

2 slices fresh ginger, grated

2 cloves garlic, crushed

1 onion, finely chopped

2 teaspoons fresh lemon or lime juice

1 teaspoon ground turmeric

1 teaspoon sugar

1 Lay fish fillets in a baking dish in a single layer.

2 Combine chillies, ginger, garlic, onion, lemon juice, turmeric and sugar.

3 Spread mixture over fish fillets, cover with foil. Bake in moderate oven for 30 minutes or until fish is tender.

SERVES 4

❖ **GARLIC STORAGE**

Simply blend fresh garlic with a little white vinegar and store in an airtight jar in the fridge. Use whenever crushed garlic is required in a recipe - saves time! Alternatively, store whole, peeled cloves in a jar of oil. These will keep for many months and can be crushed when needed.

INDIAN FISH CUTLETS

Mild

250 g fish fillet, cooked

250 g rice, cooked

1 teaspoon butter

2 to 4 teaspoons curry powder

3 eggs

pepper

1 cup fresh white breadcrumbs

4 tablespoons dessicated coconut

seasoned flour

oil for deep frying

1 Mince fish and rice in a food processor or blender or (chop very finely).

2 Heat butter in a small pan and sauté curry powder for 1 minute. Add to fish mixture.

3 Add 1 egg and pepper to taste and mix well. Divide mixture into 4 portions and with wet hands, shape into cutlets.

4 Beat remaining eggs and place in a shallow plate.

5 Place breadcrumbs and coconut on a sheet of greaseproof paper and stir lightly to mix. Place seasoned flour on separate sheet of greaseproof paper.

6 Coat cutlets with seasoned flour, then dip in the egg and coat with breadcrumbs. Press crumbs on lightly.

7 Heat oil and fry the cutlets for 5 minutes. Drain well. Serve with lime pickle or chutney.

SERVES 4

PRAWNS IN GARLIC AND CHILLI SAUCE

Medium

1 kg uncooked king prawns

3 cloves garlic, crushed

2 teaspoons sugar

1 teaspoon soy sauce

½ teaspoon sesame oil

2 tablespoons cornflour

5 tablespoons oil

2 teaspoons oyster sauce

2 tablespoons water

1 tablespoon ginger wine

1 tablespoon chilli sauce

1 tablespoon tomato sauce

1 large onion, chopped

1 green or red capsicum (pepper), chopped

2 spring onions, chopped

1 Peel prawns leaving tail intact, remove back vein.

2 Combine prawns in a bowl with garlic, sugar, soy sauce, sesame oil and 1 tablespoon of the cornflour. Mix well, stand 10 minutes.

3 Heat 4 tablespoons of oil in a frying pan and fry prawns for 5 minutes. Remove.

4 Combine remaining 1 tablespoon cornflour with oyster sauce, water, ginger wine, chilli sauce and tomato sauce.

5 Heat remaining 1 tablespoon oil in a saucepan, sauté onion and capsicum for 2 minutes.

6 Add prawns and cornflour mixture, stir over heat 5 minutes or until sauce has thickened. Add spring onions.

SERVES 6 TO 8

Prawns in Garlic and Chilli Sauce

PRAWNS WITH EGGS

Mild

1½ kg green prawns

2 tablespoons oil

2 medium onions, sliced

2 cloves garlic, crushed

2 green chillies, sliced and seeds removed

½ teaspoon ground black pepper

1 teaspoon ground turmeric

2 tablespoons white vinegar

2½ cups (625 ml) water

1 cup (250 ml) coconut milk

2 eggs, lightly beaten

1 Peel prawns leaving tail intact, remove back vein.

2 Heat oil in a frying pan, sauté onions, garlic and chillies for 3 minutes. Add pepper and turmeric, sauté 1 minute.

3 Add vinegar and water and half the coconut milk. Simmer uncovered, over moderate heat for 10 minutes.

4 Add prawns, simmer further 10 minutes. Shake pan occasionally to prevent sticking.

5 Add remaining coconut milk. Pour in eggs, shake the pan gently, cook further 5 minutes until the eggs are cooked.

SERVES 4 TO 6

BAKED WHOLE FISH

Mild

¼ green capsicum (pepper), chopped

½ cup chopped, fresh coriander leaves or parsley

1 teaspoon ground cumin

¼ teaspoon chilli powder

½ teaspoon ground ginger

½ teaspoon garlic salt

1 tablespoon white vinegar

1 kg whole fish

30 g butter, melted

1 Combine capsicum, coriander, cumin, chilli, ginger, garlic salt and vinegar. Spoon into cavity of fish.

2 Brush fish with butter, wrap in a piece of foil. Place into a baking dish, bake in moderate oven for 30 minutes or until tender.

SERVES 6 TO 8

COCONUT SPICED FISH

Mild

3 tablespoons oil

500 g white fish cutlets

3 onions, sliced

½ green capsicum (pepper), sliced

2 teaspoons curry powder

1¼ cups (310 ml) coconut cream

juice 1 lemon

1 Heat oil in a frying pan. Fry fish pieces on both sides until brown, remove.

2 Add onions, capsicum and curry powder to pan, sauté until onions are tender. Add the fish and coconut cream.

3 Cover, simmer until fish is cooked, stir in lemon juice.

SERVES 4

PRAWNS IN COCONUT

Mild

500 g uncooked medium-sized prawns

1 tablespoon white vinegar

½ teaspoon turmeric

3 tablespoons oil

1 teaspoon mustard seeds

1 small onion, chopped

1 clove garlic, chopped

2 fresh green chillies, finely chopped and seeds removed

2 curry leaves

thin slice ginger, finely chopped

4 tablespoons desiccated coconut

1 Peel prawns leaving tails intact, remove back vein.

2 Combine prawns in a bowl with vinegar and turmeric.

3 Heat oil in a frying pan, sauté mustard seeds for 1 minute.

4 Add onion, garlic, chillies, curry leaves and ginger, sauté for 2 minutes.

5 Add prawns, sauté for 4 minutes.

6 Add desiccated coconut, sauté further 3 minutes or until coconut is lightly browned.

SERVES 4

❖ **CURRY POWDER**

Curry powder is a blend of many spices, including: cloves, cinnamon, cardamom, cumin, chilli, ginger, coriander, turmeric, fenugreek and mustard. Make your own curry powder - experiment with varying quantities of these spices until you get the perfect blend. Keep curry powder in airtight jars.

RICE

Rice is an indispensable part of an Indian meal, an essential background to a hot, spicy spread. Plain boiled rice can be served with any of the curries or spicy dishes you make, as well as the more creative pilau and biriani dishes.

There are many types of rice - long grain is usually preferred for pilau and biriani, with short grain usually being used for creamy desserts. Long grain rice absorbs more water than short grain so this should be taken into account when cooking it. Soak rice in cold water before cooking it, to help separate the grains.

Vegetable Pilau

PLAIN BOILED RICE

3 cups (500 g) rice

water

1 Wash rice in cold water four or five times, until water is clear.

2 Add cold water to come 2 cm above rice in saucepan. Bring to the boil, reduce heat to medium. Continue cooking until water evaporates, leaving air bubble holes through rice.

3 Reduce heat to low. Place lid on saucepan and continue cooking for 10 minutes. Do not stir or lift lid during cooking time. (Another method for boiling rice is to add it to a very large pot of rapidly boiling salted water and cook at a rolling boil, uncovered for 15 to 20 minutes. Drain in a colander).

SERVES 6 TO 8

SAFFRON RICE

3 cups (500 g) long grain rice

3 tablespoons ghee

2 onions, finely sliced

1 teaspoon ground turmeric

¼ teaspoon saffron powder

5 cups (1¼ litres) hot chicken stock

½ teaspoon cracked pepper

OPTIONAL

3 tablespoons sultanas

½ cup almonds, sautéed in oil until golden brown

1 cup cooked peas

1 Wash rice in cold water, drain.

2 Melt ghee in a heavy based frying pan, sauté onion until golden.

3 Add turmeric, saffron and rice, stir well to coat rice with ghee. Fry until rice grains

Saffron Rice with sultanas, almonds and peas

are just golden, approximately 5 minutes.

4 Add stock, and pepper, stir well, bring to boil. Turn heat very low, cover pan tightly, and cook for 20 minutes. Do not lift lid or stir during cooking time.

5 Turn off heat and leave uncovered for 10 minutes to release steam. Loosen rice grains with a fork. Fold in sultanas, almonds and peas, if desired.

SERVES 4 TO 6

FISH PILAU

Medium

185 g ghee

2 large onions, sliced

1 kg fish cutlets (firm-fleshed fish should be used)

500 g (3 cups) rice

8 cardamom seeds

6 cloves

2 teaspoons red chillies, chopped and seeds removed

2 teaspoons ground coriander

1 stick cinnamon

2 teaspoons garam masala

1 Melt ghee in a frying pan, sauté onion until brown, remove.

2 Add fish cutlets, fry on each side until brown, remove.

3 Tie cardamom and cloves in a muslin bag.

4 Bring 2 litres of water to the boil, add rice, chillies, coriander, cinnamon, and the muslin bag. When the rice is cooked, drain in a colander, remove muslin bag.

5 In a 2 litre heat-proof dish, arrange a layer of rice, then a layer of fish and so on, ending with a layer of rice. Sprinkle garam masala on the top. Cover and cook in a slow oven for 15 to 20 minutes.

SERVES 8 TO 10

SAFFRON KEDGEREE

½ teaspoon cumin seeds

10 cardamom seeds

180 g ghee

15 g slivered almonds

15 g currants

3 medium onions, thinly sliced

1¼ cups (250 g rice), washed

¾ cup (120 g) lentils

4 threads saffron

1¼ cups (310 ml) coconut milk

8 green chillies, sliced and seeds removed

½ teaspoon ground ginger

10 cloves

4 small sticks cinnamon

3 tablespoons sugar

1 Coarsely grind the cumin and cardamom seeds.

2 Heat the ghee and sauté the almonds and currants till the almonds are medium brown. Remove and reserve.

3 Sauté onions in the ghee, until crisp and brown. Set onions aside, reserve ghee.

4 In a medium saucepan, put ⅔ cup water and the rice. Half cook the rice and put into a large saucepan.

5 In a medium saucepan put ⅓ cup water and lentils, cook for 20 minutes or till half done. Add this to the rice.

6 Add saffron, coconut milk, half the almonds and currants, fried onions, green chillies, ginger, cloves, cinnamon, sugar and the reserved ghee. Mix thoroughly and cover.

7 Bring to the boil and simmer till rice and lentils are cooked. Stir the kedgeree with a fork and leave on a very low heat for 5 minutes more. Serve sprinkled with remaining almonds and currants.

SERVES 4 TO 6

LAMB BIRIANI

LAMB

1 kg lamp chops

1½ tablespoons ground coriander

1 teaspoon ground paprika

¼ teaspoon ground cumin

¼ teaspoon ground aniseed

¼ teaspoon each ground turmeric, ground cinnamon, ground cardamom, ground cloves

2 teaspoons grated, fresh ginger

2 cloves garlic, crushed

1 tablespoon white vinegar

1 teaspoon fresh lemon juice

3 tablespoons oil

4 large onions, finely chopped

3 tablespoons ground almonds

6 tablespoons plain yoghurt

RICE

4 cups long grain rice, washed and drained

3 tablespoons ghee

2 onions, finely sliced

1 teaspoon grated, fresh ginger

1 clove garlic, crushed

6 cups (1½ litres) water

¼ teaspoon each ground turmeric, ground cinnamon, ground cardamom, ground cloves

1 bay leaf

4 tablespoons evaporated milk

GARNISH

1 large onion, peeled, sliced and fried golden brown

125 g cashew nuts, fried lightly

1 TO PREPARE LAMB. Remove excess fat from chops, place lamb in a bowl.

2 In another bowl, mix coriander, paprika, cumin, aniseed, turmeric, cinnamon, cardamom, cloves, ginger, garlic, vinegar and lemon juice. Add to lamb and mix well. Allow to stand for 15 minutes.

3 Heat oil in a large saucepan, sauté onions until golden brown. Add marinated meat. Cover saucepan and simmer with no added water for 40 minutes.

4 Remove from heat, add almonds and yoghurt. Stir to prevent sticking. Cook, covered, until liquid has dried up and oil rises. Remove saucepan from heat and put aside.

5 TO PREPARE RICE. In a large saucepan, melt ghee, sauté onions until golden brown. Add ginger and garlic and sauté for 2 minutes.

6 Add rice, water, turmeric, cinnamon, cardamom, cloves and bay leaf. Mix well. Bring to the boil. Boil, covered, until rice is three-quarters cooked, then reduce heat to very low. Add evaporated milk, and continue to cook until remaining liquid is absorbed. Stir rice with a fork, remove from heat.

7 Transfer half the rice to a serving dish or casserole. Spread half the curried lamb over it. Make another layer of rice, and top dish with remaining lamb.

Garnish with fried onion rings and cashew nuts.

SERVES 6 TO 8

Lamb Biriani

CHICKEN PILAU

Mild

1 teaspoon saffron threads

2 tablespoons fresh lemon juice

500 g chicken thigh fillets, cut into 2 cm cubes

4 teaspoons garam masala

2 cloves garlic, crushed

½ teaspoon ground ginger

2½ cups (625 ml) plain yoghurt

4 medium onions, sliced

2 cups (375 g) long grain rice

2 tablespoons sugar

45 g butter

1 Combine saffron with lemon juice, stand 5 minutes.

2 Sauté onion until golden brown. Set aside.

3 Combine chicken with 3 teaspoons garam masala, half of the saffron juice, garlic, ginger, 1¾ cups (430 ml) yoghurt and fried onion, leave for an hour.

4 Place mixture into a saucepan and simmer over a very low heat until chicken is tender.

5 Cook rice in boiling water until nearly ready. Drain and return to saucepan with remaining yoghurt, 1 teaspoon garam masala, sliced onions, saffron juice, sugar, butter and chicken mixture.

6 Cover and simmer over a low heat until the rice is cooked, stirring with a fork occasionally.

SERVES 4 TO 6

COCONUT RICE

3 cups (500 g) long grain rice, washed and drained

3 cups (750 ml) canned coconut milk

GARNISH

½ cup raisins

1 onion, peeled, sliced and fried golden brown

6 tablespoons slivered almonds, lightly fried

1 Put rice and coconut milk in a saucepan.

2 Bring to the boil on medium heat, and boil until liquid has evaporated and steam holes appear.

3 Reduce heat to very low. Cover and continue cooking until rice is well cooked and fluffy. Stir with a fork. Garnish with raisins, onion and almonds.

SERVES 4 TO 6

KEEMA PILAU

Mild

1 onion, finely sliced

250 g ghee

500 g lean meat, minced

1 teaspoon ground ginger

1 teaspoon chilli powder

2 teaspoons ground coriander

2 tablespoons plain yoghurt

few strands saffron

3 cups (500 g) rice

8 cloves

1 stick cinnamon

1 Sauté onion in the ghee until golden.

2 Add the mince, ginger, chilli and coriander. Sauté until mince is browned, add yoghurt and fry until rich brown.

3 Soak the saffron in 1 tablespoon water and add to the mince.

4 Combine rice, cloves and cinnamon in a large pan. Add enough water to come 6 cm above the level of the rice. Bring to the boil, cover and simmer until the water has almost evaporated and the rice nearly cooked. Remove from the heat.

5 In a 2 litre heat-proof dish, arrange in a layer of rice then a layer of mince and so on until all the mince and rice are used up. The last layer must be rice. Cover, bake in a slow oven for 20 minutes until the rice is cooked. Before serving, mix the pilau very carefully so as not to break the rice grains.

SERVES 6 TO 8

STEP-BY-STEP TECHNIQUES

MANGO PILAU

Medium

6 cups (1 kg) long grain rice

1 teaspoon salt

½ teaspoon turmeric

1 teaspoon cumin seeds

6 red chillies, chopped and seeds removed

2 cups (100 g) grated coconut

6 half-ripe mangoes, peeled and chopped

125 g ghee

3 to 4 curry leaves

2 teaspoons mustard seeds

2 red chillies, for garnish

1 Boil rice with salt and turmeric until cooked.

2 Combine cumin, 3 chillies and coconut in a food processor or blender. Mix with mangoes. Add to cooked rice with half the ghee and set aside.

3 Heat remaining ghee and sauté curry leaves, mustard seeds and other 3 chillies until mustard seeds start to pop. Combine with rice mixture. Garnish with whole red chillies.

SERVES 8 TO 10

Add cumin, chilli, coconut and mango mixture to the cooked rice

Sauté curry leaves, mustard seeds and remaining chillies in melted ghee

When mustard seeds have popped, combine mixture with rice

VEGETABLE PILAU

Mild

185 g ghee

2 medium onions, sliced

60 g cauliflower, broken into small florets

60 g potatoes, finely diced

60 g green beans, cut into 2 cm lengths

60 g shelled peas

60 g carrots, finely sliced

½ teaspoon ground turmeric

½ teaspoon ground ginger

½ teaspoon ground cardamom

1 bay leaf

4 cloves

2 teaspoons cracked pepper

1½ cups (250 g) rice

4 cups (1 litre) boiling water

1 Heat the ghee in a large saucepan and sauté the onions until golden brown. Remove and set aside.

2 Add cauliflower, potatoes, beans, peas and carrots to ghee in pan, sauté until tender. Remove and set aside.

3 Sauté turmeric, ginger, cardamom, bay leaf, cloves and pepper for 1 minute.

4 Add the rice and fry for 2 minutes, stirring all the time.

5 Add 4 cups boiling water and boil till the water is nearly gone. Turn into a heat-proof dish, add the fried vegetables, cover, bake in a slow oven 140°C (275°F) for 15 to 20 minutes. Serve with the fried onions sprinkled on top.

SERVES 6 TO 8

DATE AND LENTIL PILAU

3 cups (500 g) long grain rice

1 cup red lentils

250 g butter

1 cup (250 ml) warm water

1 small onion, finely chopped

250 g fresh dates, stoned

125 g dried apricots, chopped

½ cup blanched almonds, chopped

½ cup raisins

1 Boil rice until almost cooked.

2 Cover lentils with water and cook for 20 minutes until soft.

3 Dissolve half the butter in water over heat.

4 Sauté onion in remaining butter until soft, add dates, apricots, almonds and raisins.

5 Pour ½ butter water into casserole dish then add, in layers, ⅓ of the rice, ½ of fruit mixture, ½ of the lentils, ⅓ of the rice, remaining fruit mixture, remaining lentils, then remaining rice and pour over the remaining butter-water.

6 Cover with cloth then put lid on, simmer over low heat for 30 to 40 minutes.

SERVES 8

VEGETARIAN DISHES
AND VEGETABLE ACCOMPANIMENTS

Some of the best vegetarian food in the world can be found in India. States of Southern India are predominantly vegetarian and many delicious and nutritious dishes are found there.

In Indian cooking, vegetables are never boiled and the water then discarded. They are cooked with a little water, or with some other liquid which forms the sauce of the dish, so that the nutrients are retained, or in a dry style such as bhajis.

In this section you will find recipes using all kinds of vegetables, and various ways of cooking them. Serve these dishes as a meal on their own with some rice, or serve as accompaniments to a meat meal. Whip up a cool salad in hot weather, or a hot vegetable curry in the cold winter months.

Clockwise from top left: Okra Bhujia, Stuffed Tomatoes, Cottage Cheese Salad, Banana and Coconut, Cucumber, Onion and Celery Salad, Pumpkin and Mustard Salad, Vegetable Salad

MUGHAL VEGETABLES

Mild

3 tablespoons oil

2 onions, sliced

seeds from 6 cardamom pods

5 cm stick cinnamon, broken

2 tablespoons poppy seeds

¾ teaspoon chilli powder

¼ teaspoon ground cloves

250 g cauliflower florets

250 g zucchini (courgettes), sliced

175 g carrots, sliced

175 g green beans, sliced

100 g mushrooms, sliced

⅓ cup (30 g) desiccated coconut

¼ cup (30 g) slivered almonds

¼ cup (60 g) pistachio nuts (optional)

2 cups (500 ml) stock

⅔ cup (160 ml) sour cream

2 teaspoons fresh lemon juice

1 Heat oil in a large saucepan and sauté onion until soft but not brown.

2 Add spices, vegetables, coconut, nuts and stock and season to taste. Bring to boil, cover and simmer for 15 minutes until vegetables are tender.

3 Using a slotted spoon, transfer vegetables to a serving dish and keep warm. Add sour cream and lemon juice to liquid, reheat and spoon over vegetables.

SERVES 4

Mughal Vegetables

STEP-BY-STEP TECHNIQUES

LOUDOU'S INDIAN VEGETABLE CURRY

Mild

⅓ cup (80 ml) oil

2 teaspoons ground cumin

½ teaspoon ground turmeric

¼ teaspoon chilli powder

2 large onions, chopped

2 cloves garlic, crushed

small piece ginger, grated

2 large tomatoes, peeled and chopped

4 potatoes, quartered

small head cauliflower, broken into florets

3 to 4 zucchini (courgettes), chopped

½ eggplant (aubergine), chopped

½ cup (125 ml) water

1 cup peas

1 Heat oil, stir in cumin, turmeric, chilli powder.. Add onions, garlic and ginger and sauté, stirring until onions are soft but not brown. Add all vegetables except peas and cook, stirring for 5 minutes.

2 Add water, cover and simmer over low heat for 20 minutes. Add peas and simmer 5 minutes more. Most of the moisture should be absorbed during cooking.

SERVES 4

Loudou's Indian Vegetable Curry

Fry onions, garlic and ginger with curry spices

Add remaining vegetables except peas

Add water and simmer over a low heat

CHITCHKEE

Mild to Medium

500 g mixed raw vegetables (peas, carrots, beans, turnip, cauliflower or potatoes)

2 tablespoons ghee

1 onion, sliced

2 cloves garlic, sliced

2 to 4 tablespoons curry powder

250 g tomatoes, peeled and chopped

1 cup (250 ml) water

1 Cut vegetables into even bite-sized pieces.

2 Melt ghee in a saucepan, sauté onion, garlic and curry powder until onion is tender.

3 Add tomatoes, water and vegetables, bring to the boil. Cover, reduce heat to low, simmer for 15 minutes or until vegetables are tender.

SERVES 4

❖ **CHICKPEAS**

The best way to remove the skins from chickpeas is to rub them in a cloth after soaking them overnight.

If you don't have time to soak chickpeas overnight, buy them canned (also called garbanzos) in Asian food stores and use these in any recipe requiring chickpeas. Add them towards the end of the cooking time as they only need heating through

MIXED VEGETABLE CURRY

Medium

200 g carrots, cut into 2 cm lengths

200 g beans, cut into 3 cm lengths

100 g peas, shelled

200 g pumpkin, cut into 2 cm cubes

1 tablespoon split peas

1 cup (250 ml) plain yoghurt

¼ cup (60 ml) water

3 tablespoons desiccated coconut

3 green chillies, chopped and seeds removed

2 teaspoons cumin seeds

30 g ghee

8 curry leaves

1 Cook carrots, beans, peas and pumpkin separately in boiling water until tender, drain.

2 Place split peas in a frying pan, stir over low heat 5 minutes. Put split peas in a bowl, cover with water and stand 1 hour. Drain and crush to a paste (dhal).

3 Combine vegetables and dhal in a saucepan with yoghurt, water, coconut, chillies and cumin. Cook over low heat, without boiling for 10 minutes.

4 Melt ghee in a frying pan and sauté curry leaves until lightly browned, spoon over vegetable curry to serve.

SERVES 4

POTATOES WITH CHICKPEAS

Mild

250 g chickpeas

2 large potatoes

60 g ghee

2 onions, sliced

2 teaspoons fresh ginger, grated

1 teaspoon ground turmeric

½ teaspoon chilli powder

1 teaspoon ground coriander

½ teaspoon garam masala

3 tablespoons fresh lemon juice

1 Place chickpeas in a bowl, cover with water, stand overnight.

2 Drain chickpeas, place in a saucepan, cover with water, bring to the boil. Reduce heat to low, cover, simmer for 1 hour or until tender, drain.

3 Cook potatoes in boiling water until tender. Drain, peel and cut into pieces.

4 Melt ghee, in a frying pan, add onions, ginger, turmeric, chilli and coriander, sauté until tender.

5 Add chickpeas, potatoes, garam masala and lemon juice, stir over low heat until heated through.

SERVES 2 TO 4

POTATO CURRY

Potato Curry

Mild

60 g ghee

500 g potatoes, cut into 3 cm cubes

1 teaspoon ground turmeric

1 teaspoon ground cumin

250 g tomatoes, chopped

1 teaspoon chilli powder

hot water

1 Melt ghee in a saucepan, add potatoes, turmeric and cumin, sauté 5 minutes.

2 Add tomatoes, chilli powder and enough hot water to cover the potatoes. Bring to the boil, cover, reduce heat to low. Simmer about 15 minutes or until potatoes are tender.

SERVES 4 TO 6

SPINACH AND POTATO CURRY

Mild

60 g ghee

1 large onion, sliced

250 g potatoes, quartered

1 teaspoon ground cumin

2 green chillies, finely chopped and seeds removed

½ teaspoon ground ginger

½ cup (125 ml) water

1 kg spinach leaves, roughly chopped

1 Melt ghee in a saucepan, sauté onion until tender.

2 Add potatoes, cumin, chillies, ginger and water. Cover, cook over low heat 5 minutes, stir occasionally.

3 Add spinach, cover, cook for 2 minutes. Uncover pan, simmer until water has evaporated. Replace lid, cook over very low heat for 20 minutes or until potato is tender.

SERVES 6 TO 8

❖ **STAR ANISE**

The star-shaped flowers come from a tree which grows in parts of Asia. The flowers are made up of segments which each contain one seed. You can buy the hard, dried fruits or ready ground star anise. Store the ground anise in airtight jars to retain its flavour

SPICY CAULIFLOWER

Mild

2 tablespoons oil

1 large onion, sliced

3 star anise

1 teaspoon freshly ground pepper

½ teaspoon ground turmeric

500 g cauliflower, broken into florets

¼ cup (60 ml) water

1 tablespoon fresh lemon juice

1 Heat oil in a saucepan, add onion and star anise, sauté until onion is tender.

2 Add pepper, turmeric, cauliflower, water and lemon juice. Cover and bring to the boil. Reduce heat to low, simmer for 5 minutes or until cauliflower is tender.

SERVES 4

CAULIFLOWER KOFTAS IN TOMATO SAUCE

Mild

SAUCE

12 large, ripe tomatoes, chopped

1 tablespoon brown sugar

1 bay leaf

1 tablespoon paprika

30 g butter

1 tablespoon chopped fresh basil

KOFTAS

1 large cauliflower, roughly chopped

¾ cup chickpea flour (also called besan flour)

2 teaspoons ground cumin

2 teaspoons ground coriander

1 teaspoon ground turmeric

¼ teaspoon ground ginger

½ teaspoon ground fenugreek

½ teaspoon cayenne pepper

1 egg, lightly beaten

250 g ghee

1 TO MAKE SAUCE: Blend or process tomatoes until smooth. Place in a saucepan and add sugar, bay leaf, paprika, butter and basil. Bring to boil, simmer uncovered until sauce has reduced and thickened.

2 TO MAKE KOFTAS: Blend or process cauliflower until finely chopped. Add flour, cumin, coriander, turmeric, ginger, fenugreek, cayenne and egg. Mix until combined, roll into walnut-sized balls.

3 Melt ghee in a frying pan, fry cauliflower balls on all sides, until firm and dark brown. Remove and drain on absorbent paper. Serve with hot tomato sauce.

SERVES 6 TO 8

CAULIFLOWER IN YOGHURT

Mild

3 onions, finely sliced

2 cloves garlic, crushed

1 teaspoon grated, fresh ginger

1 teaspoon sugar

1 cup (250 ml) plain yoghurt

1 large cauliflower, broken into florets

45 g ghee

⅔ cup (160 ml) hot water

1 teaspoon garam masala

1 Combine one onion in a blender or food processor with garlic, ginger, sugar and yoghurt.

2 Blend until smooth.

3 Combine cauliflower and yoghurt mixture, stand for at least 2 hours.

4 Melt ghee in a saucepan, sauté remaining onions until golden brown.

5 Add cauliflower mixture and hot water. Cover, simmer over low heat for 15 minutes or until cauliflower is tender. Stir in garam masala.

Serves 6 to 8

Cauliflower in Yoghurt

Eggplant and Green Capsicum Curry

STUFFED TOMATOES

Mild

6 medium firm tomatoes

1 small onion, finely chopped

1 clove garlic, crushed

30 g ghee

125 g minced chicken

1 teaspoon curry powder

1 Cut a slice from the top of each tomato to form a lid, scoop out some of the inside and reserve.

2 Melt ghee in a frying pan, sauté onion and garlic until tender.

3 Add minced chicken and curry powder, sauté for 5 minutes or until brown. Add reserved tomato pulp.

4 Spoon mixture into tomato cases, replace lid and place onto a baking tray. Bake in oven 30 minutes or until tomato case is cooked but still retains its shape.

SERVES 6

EGGPLANT AND GREEN CAPSICUM CURRY

Mild

90 g ghee

1 large onion, sliced

500 g eggplant (aubergine), cut into 3 cm cubes

1 teaspoon ground turmeric

¼ teaspoon ground ginger

250 g tomatoes, quartered

2 green capsicums (peppers), sliced

1 teaspoon garam masala

1 Melt ghee in a frying pan, sauté onion until brown. Add eggplant, turmeric and ginger, sauté for 5 minutes.

2 Add tomatoes and capsicum, cover and cook over low heat for 15 minutes or until eggplant is tender.

3 Add garam masala, cook for 2 minutes.

SERVES 6 TO 8

ZUCCHINI AND POTATOES

Mild

500 g zucchini (courgettes)

4 potatoes, cut into 2 cm cubes

4 tablespoons oil

1 onion, finely chopped

1 clove garlic, chopped

1 teaspoon ground paprika

¼ teaspoon ground turmeric

¼ teaspoon ground cumin

¼ teaspoon ground cinnamon

¼ teaspoon ground cloves

¼ teaspoon ground cardamom

1 tomato, finely chopped

2 spring onions, chopped

1 Slice zucchinis lengthways, then crossways into 2 cm lengths.

2 Cook potatoes in boiling water until tender, drain.

3 Heat oil in a frying pan, sauté onions until golden brown.

4 Add, potatoes, zucchinis, garlic, paprika, turmeric, cumin, cinnamon, cloves and cardamom. Stir over low heat for 10 minutes.

5 Add tomato and spring onions, continue frying for 5 minutes or until zucchini is tender, stirring frequently to prevent burning.

SERVES 6

CABBAGE IN COCONUT

Mild

2 tablespoons oil

1 large onion, chopped

1 clove garlic, crushed

½ teaspoon ground mustard

¼ teaspoon ground cumin

¼ teaspoon ground turmeric

10 cabbage leaves, thinly sliced

2 fresh green chillies, chopped and seeds removed

2 curry leaves

2 tablespoons desiccated coconut

1 Heat oil in frying pan, sauté onion until tender.

2 Add garlic, mustard, cumin, turmeric, cabbage, chillies, curry leaves and coconut. Cover and cook over low heat 5 minutes.

3 Remove lid, stir over heat for 10 minutes or until cabbage is tender.

SERVES 4

OKRA BHUJIA

Mild

A 'Bhujia' is a very dry vegetable curry.

90 g ghee

1 onion, sliced

500 g okra, cut into small pieces

1 teaspoon ground turmeric

1 Melt ghee in a saucepan, sauté onion until tender.

2 Add okra and turmeric, sauté 1 minute. Cover, cook over very low heat for about 20 minutes or until okra is tender, stirring occasionally.

SERVES 4

CABBAGE AND CARROT BHUJIA

Medium

4 tablespoons oil

1 tablespoon whole black mustard seeds

1 dried red chilli

1 cabbage, finely sliced

350 g carrots, coarsely grated

1 green chilli, cut into thin strips and seeds removed

½ teaspoon sugar

4 tablespoons chopped, fresh coriander

1 tablespoon fresh lemon juice

1 Heat oil in a frying pan, sauté mustard seeds and dried red chilli 1 minute.

2 Add cabbage, carrots and green chilli. Reduce heat to low, stir-fry the vegetables for about 30 seconds.

3 Add sugar and coriander, stir fry for another 5 minutes or until vegetables are tender.

4 Add lemon juice. Remove red chilli before serving.

SERVES 4 TO 6

MUSHROOM BHUJIA

Mild

2 large onions, thinly sliced

125 g ghee

1 teaspoon ground turmeric

1 teaspoon chilli powder

1 clove garlic, chopped

375 g mushrooms, sliced

1 Melt ghee in a saucepan, sauté onions 3 minutes or until tender.
2 Add turmeric, chilli and garlic, sauté 1 minute.
3 Add mushrooms, sauté over low heat or until mushrooms are ready.

SERVES 4

LEEK BHUJIA

Mild

60 g ghee

1 teaspoon cumin seeds

1 kg leeks, sliced

1 teaspoon ground turmeric

½ teaspoon ground ginger

½ teaspoon garam masala

1 Melt ghee in a saucepan, sauté cumin seeds 1 minute.
2 Add leeks, turmeric and ginger, sauté 3 minutes. Cover and cook over very low heat till leeks are tender. Stir in garam masala.

SERVES 6 TO 8

FRENCH BEANS BHUJIA

Mild

60 g ghee

1 onion, chopped

750 g French beans, cut into 2 cm lengths

1 teaspoon ground turmeric

½ teaspoon chilli powder

½ teaspoon garam masala

1 Melt ghee in a saucepan, sauté onion 2 minutes.
2 Add beans, turmeric and chilli, sauté 3 minutes.
3 Add garam masala, cover and cook over very low heat for about 15 minutes or until beans are tender.

SERVES 4 TO 6

INDIAN SAVOURY OMELETTE

Mild

30 g ghee

1 small onion, finely chopped

1 green chilli, finely chopped and seeds removed

2 eggs, lightly beaten

pinch mixed herbs

1 Melt ghee in a small frying pan, sauté onion and chilli over low heat until tender.
2 Add eggs and herbs, cook without stirring, over low heat until set and lightly browned underneath.
3 Place pan under preheated grill for 2 minutes or until omelette is set on top. Fold in half to serve.

SERVES 1

BAKED SPICED EGGS

Mild

60 g ghee

2 large onions, thinly sliced

2 cloves garlic, crushed

¼ green capsicum (pepper), chopped

¼ cup chopped, fresh coriander

4 eggs, lightly beaten

1 tablespoon white vinegar

1 teaspoon sugar

½ teaspoon ground cumin

1 Melt ghee in a frying pan, sauté onions until tender.

2 Add garlic, capsicum and coriander, sauté 2 minutes. Remove from heat.

3 Add eggs, vinegar, sugar and cumin. Stir until combined.

4 Spoon into a 1 litre oven-proof dish. Bake in moderate oven for 20 minutes or until eggs have set.

SERVES 2

MADRAS EGG CURRY

Madras Egg Curry

Mild

6 hard-boiled eggs, cooled

60 g ghee

1 onion, chopped

1 clove garlic, sliced

1 tablespoon curry powder

250 g fresh tomatoes

1 tablespoon fresh lemon juice

½ cup (125 ml) water

1 Peel eggs and cut in halves lengthways.

2 Melt ghee in a frying pan, sauté onion and garlic until onion is tender. Add curry powder, sauté 1 minute.

3 Add tomatoes, lemon juice and water and bring to boil. Reduce heat to low, cover, simmer for 10 minutes.

4 Add eggs, cook until heated through.

SERVES 3

ONION SALAD

3 onions, thinly sliced

2 tablespoons fresh lemon juice

4 tablespoons desiccated coconut

½ teaspoon grated, fresh ginger

½ teaspoon sugar

1 Soak the onion rings in lemon juice for about 1 hour.

2 Add coconut, ginger and sugar.

SERVES 2

TOMATO AND ONION SALAD

2 large tomatoes

8 spring onions, finely chopped

½ teaspoon sugar

4 tablespoons plain yoghurt

1 tablespoon fresh lemon juice

1 red chilli, finely chopped and seeds removed

1 Blanch tomatoes in boiling water for 30 seconds, peel off skin, chop tomatoes roughly.

2 Combine tomatoes with spring onions, sugar, yoghurt, lemon juice and chilli.

SERVES 2

CUCUMBER, ONION AND CELERY SALAD

Mild

1 large cucumber, peeled and sliced

1 large onion, finely sliced

3 stalks celery, finely chopped

1 tablespoon chilli sauce

1 Combine cucumber, onion, celery and chilli sauce. Serve cold.

SERVES 4

❖ **CHILLI SAUCE**

Buy ready made chilli sauce from supermarkets. There are many varieties to choose from. Some may have garlic, some honey, some will be hot and some mild. Make sure you read the ingredients and find out if its the one you want.

CHOKO SALAD

Mild

2 large chokos

1 small onion, finely chopped

½ teaspoon sugar

¼ teaspoon paprika

⅔ cup (160 ml) plain yoghurt

a few coriander leaves

1 Peel the chokos under running water to prevent the gum from staining your hands. Cut into quarters, remove seeds.

2 Grate chokos, place into a strainer, press out moisture.

3 Combine chokos with onion, sugar, paprika and yoghurt. Serve with coriander.

SERVES 2 TO 4

VEGETABLE SALAD

Mild

6 lettuce leaves, thinly sliced

1 cucumber, peeled and diced

2 tomatoes, cut into wedges

2 boiled potatoes, cut into 2½ cm cubes

2 hard-boiled eggs, thickly sliced

1 carrot, coarsely grated

SAUCE

2 tablespoons crunchy peanut butter

½ teaspoon brown sugar

1 tablespoon fresh lime juice

4 tablespoons mild chilli sauce

1 teaspoon soy sauce

1 Combine lettuce, cucumber, tomatoes, potatoes, eggs and carrot in a salad bowl.

2 Blend sauce ingredients and pour over vegetables.

SERVES 4 TO 6

PUMPKIN AND MUSTARD SALAD

Mild

This dish can be varied by using sliced bananas, tomatoes, cucumbers, or boiled cauliflower florets

250 g pumpkin, peeled and sliced

¼ green capsicum (pepper), finely chopped

½ teaspoon dry mustard

¼ teaspoon ground ginger

½ teaspoon ground cumin

⅔ cup (150 ml) plain yoghurt

1 Cook pumpkin in boiling water until tender, drain.

2 Combine capsicum, mustard, ginger, cumin and yoghurt. Add pumpkin and stir well.

SERVES 4 TO 6

COTTAGE CHEESE SALAD

2 onions, thinly sliced

1 teaspoon salt

2 tablespoons desiccated coconut

4 tablespoons milk, heated

500 g cottage cheese

½ green capsicum (pepper), chopped

2 tablespoons chopped fresh coriander

3 tablespoons fresh lemon juice

¼ teaspoon freshly ground pepper

1 Sprinkle onion slices with salt and rub in with hands, stand 30 minutes. Rinse under cold water, drain.

2 Soak coconut in hot milk, stand 30 minutes.

3 Combine onions, coconut, cottage cheese, capsicum, coriander, lemon juice and pepper. Serve cold.

SERVES 4 TO 6

Pumpkin and Mustard Salad

STEP-BY-STEP TECHNIQUES

MIXED FRUIT CURRY

This curry can be served hot or cold with rice

4 to 5 pieces crystallised ginger

hot water

2 onions, chopped

60 g butter

1 teaspoon crushed coriander seeds

1 tablespoon curry powder

1 tablespoon plain flour

2 cups (500 ml) chicken stock

2 teaspoons lemon juice

freshly ground black pepper

3 cups grated coconut

4 to 5 cups chopped mixed fruits (melons, peaches, plums, grapes, bananas, apples, pears)

2 to 3 tablespoons cream

1 Cover ginger with hot water for a few minutes to remove sugar. Drain, pat dry and chop.

2 Sauté onions in butter until tender.

3 Stir in ginger, coriander seeds, curry powder and flour and cook gently for 5 minutes.

4 Gradually add stock, stirring rapidly. Bring to boil, add lemon juice and season to taste. Simmer for 30 minutes.

5 Stir in coconut, fruits and cream.

SERVES 4

Add soaked ginger to coriander seeds, curry powder, flour and onions

Slowly add stock, always stirring

Stir in coconut, mixed fruit and cream and serve

APPLE AND ONION BAKE

6 onions, sliced

2 tablespoons ghee

2 tomatoes, thickly sliced

½ cup breadcumbs

4 apples, peeled and sliced

2 green chillies, finely chopped and seeds removed

2 tablespoons chopped coriander

1 cup (250 ml) stock, heated

1 Lightly sauté onions in 1 tablespoon ghee. Remove with slotted spoon.

2 Sauté tomatoes. Drain off juices through strainer and reserve.

3 Sauté breadcrumbs in remaining ghee to brown lightly.

4 Grease baking dish and arrange onion, apple and tomato in alternate layers.

5 Put chillies, coriander and reserved juices into hot stock and pour over vegetables. Sprinkle breadcrumbs over top.

6 Cover and bake at 190°C (375°F) for 30 minutes. Uncover and cook another 15 minutes.

SERVES 4

CURRIED PEACHES

2 tablespoons butter

½ red capsicum (pepper), sliced

½ green capsicum (pepper), sliced

1 tablespoon plain flour

1 tablespoon curry powder

1 cup (250 ml) milk

8 peaches, peeled, halved and stoned

¼ teaspoon paprika

2 bananas, sliced

chopped chives, for garnish

1 Melt butter and sauté both capsicums.

2 Stir in flour and curry powder. Cook for 2 minutes, while stirring.

3 Pour in milk gradually, stirring rapidly until it comes to the boil.

4 Add peaches and paprika and simmer for 20 minutes until peaches are tender. Add bananas and heat through.

5 Sreve on a bed of white rice, sprinkled with chives.

SERVES 4

Apple and Onion Bake

SAMOSAS
AND ACCOMPANIMENTS

No Indian meal is complete without a selection of accompaniments. A meal should include a yoghurt-based side dish and a sambal or two. Raitas are very refreshing with their fruity flavour.

The recipes in this section can also be used as entrées and as 'finger food' for cocktail parties. Serve samosas (either meat or vegetable), pakoras, or fritters with a selection of sambals and yoghurt dips. Or you could just make them as an ideal snack for between meals.

The sambals and other accompaniments are very simple to make and should be made freshly for each meal. Banana and coconut, cucumber and yoghurt - just some of the interesting combinations which stimulate the taste buds and enhance the flavour of the rest of the meal.

Samosas with Meat, and
Samosas with Potato Stuffing

Prawn Fritters

PRAWN FRITTERS

500 g small cooked prawns, shelled

½ cup (60 g) rice flour

½ cup (60 g) self-raising flour

1 tablespoon cornflour

1 teaspoon baking powder

½ cup (90 g) semolina flour

½ cup (60 g) besan (chickpea flour)

1 large onion, finely chopped

thin slice ginger, finely chopped

½ capsicum (pepper), finely chopped

3 spring onions, chopped

¼ teaspoon ground turmeric

¼ teaspoon ground cumin

¼ teaspoon chilli powder

2 eggs, beaten

water as required for mixing

1 cup (250 ml) oil

1 Combine prawns in a bowl with rice flour, self-raising flour, cornflour, baking powder, semolina flour, besan, onion, ginger, capsicum, spring onions, turmeric, cumin and chilli powder.

2 Add beaten eggs and sufficient water to make a thick batter. Allow to stand for 15 minutes.

3 Heat oil in a frying pan over moderate heat. Drop tablespoons of batter, a few at a time, into the oil and fry on both sides until golden brown. Drain on absorbent paper. Serve hot, with tomato sauce or chilli sauce as a dip.

MAKES 15 TO 20

VEGETABLE AND POTATO FRITTERS

2 cups (250 g) besan (chickpea flour)

½ cup (60 g) self-raising flour

2 tablespoons cornflour

3 tablespoons rice flour

1 teaspoon baking powder

1 large potato, coarsely grated

1 large carrot, coarsely grated

1 large onion, chopped

¼ teaspoon chilli powder

¼ teaspoon ground cumin

¼ teaspoon ground turmeric

3 spring onions, finely chopped

1 tablespoon fresh lemon juice

1½ cups (375 ml) oil

1 cup (250 ml) water, approximately

1 In a bowl, combine besan, self-raising flour, cornflour, rice flour and baking powder.

2 Add potato, carrot, onion, chilli, cumin, turmeric, spring onions, lemon juice, 1 tablespoon of the oil and enough water to mix to a thick batter. Stand for 5 minutes.

3 Heat remaining oil in a frying pan over moderate heat. Drop batter, 1 tablespoon at a time, into the oil and fry on both sides until golden brown. Drain on absorbent paper. Serve hot, with chutney, chilli sauce or tomato sauce.

MAKES 20

❖ **BESAN FLOUR**

This is usually made from dried chickpeas but can be made from dried split peas too. It is an excellent source of protein and iron. It should be stored in an airtight container and usually keeps well for a few months.

PAKORAS

Use any vegetables you choose such as thinly sliced potato or eggplant, cauliflower broken into florets, spinach leaves, or chopped onion

BASIC BATTER

250 g besan (chickpea flour)

¼ teaspoon baking powder

½ teaspoon ground turmeric

1 teaspoon ground coriander

½ teaspoon chilli powder

water

1 TO MAKE BATTER: Sift besan, baking powder, turmeric, coriander and chilli into a bowl. Gradually stir in sufficient water to mix to a thick batter consistency.

2 To make pakoras, dip vegetable pieces into batter, deep fry in moderately heated oil until golden brown, drain on absorbent paper.

CORN FRITTERS

2 cups grated corn (fresh or canned)

1 cup (125 g) besan flour

2 green chillies, finely chopped
and seeds removed

½ teaspoon ground turmeric

1 teaspoon ground coriander

2 tablespoons chopped coriander

oil for deep frying

1 Combine all ingredients to make a fairly
thick batter.

2 Add a tablespoon of hot oil to the
mixture. Deep fry a tablespoon of the batter
at a time in hot oil until it is golden brown.

MAKES 15 TO 20

POTATO SAMOSAS

PASTRY

2 cups (500 g) plain flour

½ teaspoon baking powder

1 teaspoon salt

30 g ghee, melted

4 tablespoons plain yoghurt

FILLING

60 g ghee

1 small onion, chopped

500 g boiled potatoes, cut into 1 cm cubes

2 green chillies, finely chopped and seeds
removed

1 teaspoon garam masala

oil for deep frying

❖ **FRITTERS**

*Fritters should always be
served hot immediately
after cooking, and cannot
be reheated. Serve them
with a selection of
chutneys*

Samosas

1 To Make Pastry: Sift flour, baking powder and salt into a bowl. Add ghee and yoghurt, stir until combined. Knead until dough is smooth.

2 To Make Filling: Melt ghee in a frying pan, sauté onion 2 minutes.

3 Add potatoes and chillies, sauté 5 minutes. Stir in garam masala, allow to cool.

4 Take walnut-size pieces of dough, roll out on a floured surface, making thin rounds the size of a saucer.

5 Cut the rounds in half, fold each half into a cone shape, seal sides of cone with water and fill with potato mixture. Seal open end with water.

6 Deep fry samosas in moderately hot oil until golden brown, drain on absorbent paper.

MAKES 15 TO 20

SAMOSAS WITH MEAT

1 onion, finely chopped

2 cloves garlic, crushed

30 g ghee

375 g mince steak

2 teaspoons ground coriander

½ teaspoon ground ginger

½ teaspoon chilli powder

1 teaspoon garam masala

1 Melt ghee in a frying pan, sauté onion and garlic until onion is tender.

2 Add mince, coriander, ginger, chilli and garam masala. Sauté 10 minutes or until mince is well browned, cool.

3 Fill samosas as in the preceding recipe, and deep fry until golden brown. Drain on absorbent paper.

MAKES 15 TO 20

SPICED YOGHURT

1½ tablespoons oil

1 teaspoon mustard seeds

¼ teaspoon ground fenugreek

1 small onion, finely chopped

2 cloves garlic, finely chopped

2 dry red chillies, roughly chopped

¼ teaspoon ground cumin

1 fresh green chilli, finely chopped and seeds removed

3 curry leaves

2 cups (500 ml) plain yoghurt

1 Heat oil in a frying pan, add mustard seeds, fenugreek and onion, sauté until golden brown.

2 Add garlic, dry chillies, cumin, green chilli and curry leaves, sauté 1 minute.

3 Remove from heat, stir in yoghurt. Refrigerate until cold.

SERVES 4 TO 6

YOGHURT WITH WALNUTS AND FRESH CORIANDER

2 cups (500 ml) plain yoghurt

2 tablespoons finely chopped, fresh coriander

½ fresh green chilli, finely chopped

freshly ground black pepper

1 spring onion, finely sliced

60 g walnuts, roughly chopped

1 Combine yoghurt with all the other ingredients in a bowl.

SERVES 6

YOGHURT WITH CUCUMBER AND MINT

2 cups (500 ml) plain yoghurt

1 cucumber, peeled and coarsely grated

2 tablespoons finely chopped, fresh mint

½ teaspoon ground cumin

¼ teaspoon cayenne pepper

freshly ground black pepper

1 Combine all ingredients in a bowl.

SERVES 6

CUCUMBER AND YOGHURT

2 cups (500 ml) plain yoghurt

1 cucumber, finely chopped

4 spring onions, finely chopped

1 fresh red chilli, finely chopped and seeds removed

1 teaspoon grated lemon rind

1 Combine all ingredients in a bowl.

SERVES 6

Eggplant and Tomatoes,
Carrot Raita

CUCUMBER AND PINEAPPLE SALAD

1 large cucumber, peeled and sliced

1 cup canned crushed pineappple, with syrup

1 small onion, finely chopped

1 green chilli, chopped finely

1 In a bowl, combine cucumber, pineapple with syrup, onion and chillies.
2 Chill and serve.

SERVES 2 TO 4

GRILLED EGGPLANT

500 g eggplant (aubergine)

¼ cup (60 ml) olive oil

30 g ghee

1 onion, chopped

½ teaspoon ground cumin

2 green chillies, finely chopped and seeds removed

1 Cut eggplants lengthways in half, brush all over with oil. Place them skin side up under a preheated grill, cook on high heat until skin is brown.
2 Allow eggplants to cool, scoop out flesh, chop roughly, discard skin.
3 Melt ghee in a frying pan, sauté onions until tender. Add cumin, chillies and eggplant. Sauté until eggplant is tender.

SERVES 4 TO 6

EGGPLANT AND TOMATOES

500 g eggplant (aubergine), cut into 3 cm cubes.

2 teaspoons salt

60 g ghee

2 onions, chopped

1 clove garlic, crushed

½ teaspoon chilli powder

1 bay leaf

1 stick cinnamon, about 2 to 3 cm long

½ teaspoon ground black pepper

500 g tomatoes, peeled and quartered

4 tablespoons water

1 Sprinkle eggplant pieces with salt, stand 30 minutes. Rinse under cold water, drain.

2 Melt ghee in a frying pan, sauté onions until tender. Add garlic, chilli, bay leaf, cinnamon, and black pepper, sauté 2 minutes.

3 Add tomatoes and sauté 5 minutes.

4 Add water, cover, simmer over low heat until eggplant is tender, but firm.

SERVES 4 TO 6

CARROT RAITA

1 tablespoon oil

½ teaspoon mustard seeds

½ teaspoon chilli powder

3 large carrots, grated

2 tablespoons fresh lemon juice

1 Heat oil in a frying pan, add mustard seeds, sauté 1 minute.

2 Add chilli, carrot and lemon juice, sauté 1 minute, remove from heat. Serve at room temperature.

SERVES 4 TO 6

MIXED FRUIT RAITA

2 cups (500 ml) plain yoghurt

2 tablespoons cream

½ mango, diced

½ banana, diced

1 slice pineapple, diced

1 tablespoon mint, finely chopped

1 Whip yoghurt and cream together until smooth. Mix in remaining ingredients. Chill thoroughly.

SERVES 6

MANGO RAITA

2 cups (500 ml) full cream yoghurt

2 mangoes, diced

30 g ghee

1 tablespoon mustard seeds

2 red chillies, finely chopped and seeds removed

½ teaspoon fenugreek seeds

chopped coriander for garnish

1 Combine mangoes and yoghurt in a bowl.

2 Heat ghee in a frying pan, fry mustard seeds, chillies and fenugreek for 2 minutes or until they start to crackle.

3 Strain ghee and discard seeds. Stir ghee into yoghurt mixture. Garnish with coriander.

SERVES 6

BANANA RAITA

2 cups (500 ml) full cream yoghurt

1 teaspoon garam masala

2 green chillies, finely chopped and seeds removed

3 bananas, chopped

2 teaspoons ghee

1 teaspoon mustard seeds

chopped coriander for garnish

1 Combine yoghurt, garam masala, chillies and bananas.

2 Heat ghee in a small saucepan, fry mustard seeds for 2 minutes or until they begin to crackle.

3 Stir ghee into yoghurt mixture. Garnish with coriander.

SERVES 6

❖ **BANANA AND COCONUT**

For a very simple but satisfying side dish, sprinkle some lemon juice over sliced bananas, stir well, then cover with desiccated coconut.

SAMBALS

Sambals are amongst the many accompaniments you will find with an Indian meal. You can make a sambal with anything at all - various fresh or canned vegetables and fruit, seafood and eggs. You will find a wide range of sambals in this section and you can make your own cominations too.

A common ingredient of all sambals is chilli. Experiment with various quantities and find out how hot you like it! If you are serving a very hot sambal, don't forget to serve a cool yoghurt-based accompaniment too. If you have mistakenly put too much chilli in a sambal, add extra lemon juice to take some of the 'bite' out .

Serve sambals as accompaniments to a gourmet Indian spread, or serve them as starters to a Western style meal. Use them at parties together with a selection of breads, or simply with raw chopped vegetables.

Anti-clockwise from the top: Haricot Bean Sambal, Banana Sambal, Mixed Vegetable Sambal, Potato Sambal, Apple Sambal, Egg Sambal, Tomato Sambal

SAMBAL SAUCE

❖ **APPLE OR BANANA SAMBAL**

For an alternative to the recipes given here, simply mix either diced apple or sliced banana with the Sambal Sauce.

This creamy piquant sauce is made with coconut milk. Vary quantities to taste.

1 cup (250 ml) coconut milk

1 small onion, finely chopped

1 clove garlic, crushed

¼ teaspoon chilli powder

1 Combine all ingredients.

SERVES 4

Prawn Sambal

SAMBAL DRESSING

2 tablespoon oil

1 large onion, finely chopped

1 clove garlic, chopped

2 green chillies, finely chopped and seeds removed

½ teaspoon ground ginger

½ teaspoon ground cumin

1 teaspoon ground turmeric

1 pinch chilli powder

1 Heat oil in a frying pan, sauté onion until tender.

2 Add remaining ingredients, stir over low heat 2 minutes.

SERVES 2

PRAWN SAMBAL

This sambal can be served either hot or cold and is usually garnished with sliced hard-boiled eggs

1 quantity Sambal Dressing

250 g school prawns, peeled

2 tablespoons dessicated coconut

1 tablespoon lemon juice

1 Combine all ingredients.

SERVES 6

APPLE SAMBAL

2 green apples, diced

1 red chilli, finely chopped

2 tablespoons lemon juice

1 Combine apples, chilli and lemon juice.

SERVES 4

❖ **SERVING SAMBALS**

These sambals can be served as accompaniments or as entrées. Egg Sambal and Mixed Vegetable Sambal are good starters. The Potato Sambal is excellent served with pooris.

BUTTER OR HARICOT BEAN SAMBAL

310 g can butter beans, drained

1 red chilli, finely chopped

2 tablespoons lemon juice

1 Combine beans, chilli and lemon juice.

SERVES 4

EGG SAMBAL

This dish makes a good starter

4 hard-boiled eggs, halved lengthways

½ small onion, finely chopped

1 green chilli, finely chopped

1 tablespoon oil

1 tablespoon lemon juice

2 tablespoons desiccated coconut

1 Combine eggs, onion, chilli, oil and lemon juice.

2 Sprinkle with desiccated or fresh grated coconut, just before serving.

SERVES 4

MIXED VEGETABLE SAMBALS

2 carrots, finely diced

½ cup shelled peas

60 g green beans, cut into 1 cm lengths

1 turnip, finely diced

1 potato, finely diced

2 green chillies, finely chopped

2 tablespoons lemon juice

2 tablespoons oil

desiccated coconut

1 Cook vegetables in boiling water until tender, drain.

2 Add chillies, lemon juice and oil, stir until combined.

3 Serve sprinkled with desiccated coconut.

SERVES 4

POTATO SAMBAL

2 potatoes, cut into 1 cm cubes

1 green chilli, finely chopped

1 pinch chilli powder

2 spring onions, chopped

1 tablespoon oil

2 tablespoons lemon juice

1 Cook potatoes in boiling water until tender, drain.

2 Combine potatoes with remaining ingredients.

SERVES 4

TOMATO SAMBAL

2 ripe tomatoes, finely sliced

1 onion, finely sliced

1 to 2 green chillies, finely chopped

1 tablespoon lemon juice

freshly ground black pepper

salt

**2 tablespoons coconut
(dessicated or freshly grated)**

1 Combine tomatoes, onion, chillies, lemon juice, pepper and salt.

2 Sprinkle with desiccated or freshly grated coconut to serve.

SERVES 4

BANANA SAMBAL

2 green bananas, thinly sliced

1 red chilli, finely chopped

2 tablespoons lemon juice

1 Combine bananas, chilli and lemon juice.

SERVES 4

BREADS

There are many kinds of Indian breads some of which are unleavened and are more like a Western style pancake. They are made with a variety of grains, including rice flour and semolina. They can be plain or stuffed with various fillings. There are deep-fried breads such as poori or oven-baked ones such as naan.

Chapatis are the daily bread of millions of Indians, cooked on a griddle and eaten with every meal, or simply with a bowl of dhal. Dosa is usually stuffed with a spicy potato mixture and served with a couple of accompaniments, usually a chutney and a yoghurt dish. Or create your own filling from any vegetables or meat. They can form a meal in themselves. Parathas are also usually stuffed, and are a light tasty snack, good to serve as an entrée.

Naan is a favourite bread to eat at Indian restaurants. It is traditionally made in a tandoor oven, the dough being slapped against the sides of the oven, but you can make it in your own oven with good results. Naan is served just plain, or you can spread buttered dough with crushed garlic for a very tasty garlic naan.

Serve any of these breads with a variety of curries and accompaniments, using the bread to scoop up the food, in true Indian style. Practise this before trying it in front of your guests!

Chapatis, Vegetable Chapatis and Pappadums

VEGETABLE CHAPATIS

2½ cups (310 g) plain flour

1 onion, finely sliced

1 tablespoon finely chopped coriander leaves

½ red capsicum (pepper), finely chopped

cold water

¼ cup (60 ml) oil

1 Sift flour into a bowl.

2 Add onion, coriander and capsicum, mix well.

3 Add as much ice-cold water as required to make a soft dough.

4 Divide up into walnut sized balls. Flatten and roll out thinly.

5 Heat a frying pan, brush it with oil and fry the chapatis (they should be like thick pancakes) on both sides until brown.

MAKES 6 TO 8

DOSA

Eaten extensively in southern India, dosa originated among the poorer people who were mostly vegetarians

1½ cups (185 g) rice flour

1½ cups (185 g) plain flour

a little chilli powder (optional)

2 tablespoons plain yoghurt

1 tablespoon ghee, melted

1 Mix the rice flour with the plain flour.

2 Add chilli, yoghurt, ghee and enough water to make a thick batter. Cover and stand at least 8 hours or overnight, at room temperature.

3 Spread heaped tablespoons of mixture thinly into a greased frying pan, cook over medium heat until lightly browned, remove. Repeat with remaining mixture.

MAKES 15 TO 20

POTATO STUFFING FOR DOSA

30 g ghee

¼ teaspoon mustard seeds

1 medium onion, finely chopped

250 g potatoes, boiled, cooled, peeled and diced

¼ teaspoon turmeric

¼ teaspoon chilli powder

1 Heat the ghee and fry the mustard seeds for 1 minute.

2 Add the onion and sauté until tender.

3 Add potatoes, turmeric and chilli, sauté for 2 minutes or until dry. Put a spoonful of this mixture in each dosa, roll up like a pancake and serve.

MAKES 15

RICE PANCAKES

1½ cups (185 g) plain flour

1½ cups (185 g) rice flour

1½ teaspoons salt

3 eggs, lightly beaten

3 cups (750 ml) water

ghee

1 Sift all dry ingredients into a bowl, make a well in the centre, add eggs and water.

2 Gradually incorporate until smooth.

3 Lightly grease a frying pan with ghee. Heat to medium, pour enough batter into the pan to make a thin pancake, cover pan with a lid, cook for a few minutes. When the edges begin to lift off the pan, remove the pancake onto a plate.

4 Serve these fried side up with a filling such as mince, if desired.

MAKES 12

STEP-BY-STEP TECHNIQUES

Rub ghee into the flour

CHAPATIS

3 cups (375 g) fine wholemeal flour
1 tablespoon ghee
1 cup 250 ml) lukewarm water
oil

1 Place flour in a bowl. Rub in ghee.
2 Add water and mix into a firm dough.
3 Knead dough 10 to 15 minutes until elastic. Cover and rest for 1 hour.
4 Pinch off pieces of dough about the size of a large walnut and roll out on a lightly floured board into a thin circle.
5 Heat a little oil in a frying pan and place one chapati in pan, cook for 1 minute. Turn and cook the other side. Press lightly around the edges of chapati to encourage bread to rise a little, remove, repeat with remaining chapatis.

MAKES 6 TO 8

Pinch off walnut-sized pieces of dough and roll out to a thin circle

Fry one chapati at a time, on each side

Chapatis

COCONUT BREAD

2 tablespoons desiccated coconut

3 tablespoons plain flour

pinch cayenne pepper

¼ teaspoon sugar

60 g ghee

1 Combine coconut, flour, cayenne and sugar together. Add enough cold water to mix to a soft dough.

2 Roll out into small flat cakes.

3 Fry a few at a time in the melted ghee until cooked and light brown, drain.

MAKES 4

❖ **HORSERADISH CREAM**

Horseradish cream is grated horseradish mixed with egg and spices to a mayonnaise-like cream. It is readily available at supermarkets.

POORIS

4 cups (500 g) plain or wholemeal flour, sifted

cold water

120 g ghee

1 Combine flour with enough cold water to make a soft pliable dough, knead lightly until smooth. Cover with a damp cloth for an hour, and then knead again until the dough does not stick to the hands.

3 Make small balls the size of an egg. Roll these out on a floured board until they are the size of a small saucer.

4 Heat ghee in deep frying pan, add one poori at a time. With a flat spoon or spatula, press the poori gently until it puffs out; turn and cook until pale golden. Drain, serve hot.

MAKES 24

STUFFED PARATHAS

1 cup (125 g) plain flour, sifted

60 g butter

cold water

1 tablespoon prepared horseradish cream

1 Rub 15 g of the butter into the flour and add enough water to mix to a soft dough.

2 Divide into 8 parts. Roll out each of the 8 pieces thinly to a round shape.

3 Spread horseradish on one round and cover with another. Repeat to make 4 parathas.

4 Melt remaining butter in a frying pan, add parathas, cook on both sides over medium heat until browned and cooked through.

MAKES 4

NAAN

1¼ teaspoons dry yeast

1 cup (250 ml) lukewarm water

3 teaspoons sugar

2 tablespoons plain yoghurt

¼ cup melted ghee

1 teaspoon salt

4 cups (500 g) plain white flour

melted ghee or butter, extra

2½ tablespoons cumin seeds

1 Preheat oven to 230°C (450°F).

2 Dissolve the yeast in half the water. Mix in sugar and put mixture aside for 10 minutes, or until it starts 'frothing'.

3 Mix in yoghurt, rest of water, melted ghee and salt. Knead flour into this mixture to make a stiff dough, then knead, alternately pressing and folding, for a further 15 minutes.

4 Warm a bowl large enough to hold twice the volume of dough. Grease the bowl, and cover the dough with this. Set dough aside, until it has doubled in volume.

5 Divide dough into 10 balls. Form thick, round discs, the size of a small dinner plate. Brush the shapes of dough with melted ghee or butter, sprinkle with cumin seeds, place in preheated oven for 10 minutes or until they puff up and go a golden-brown colour.

MAKES 10

SEMOLINA POORIS

2 cups (250 g) plain flour

1 cup (125 g) semolina

½ teaspoon turmeric

¼ cup (30 g) rice flour

45 g butter

¼ cup oil

cold water

1 Mix flour, semolina and turmeric. Rub in 30 g butter.

2 Form into a soft dough with cold water, kneading the dough well.

3 Combine remaining 15 g butter with rice flour, beat until creamy.

4 Roll out the soft dough into a large circle and spread the rice flour mixture evenly on it. Roll it up and roll out again.

5 Cut into 6 cm rounds with a biscuit cutter and fry in the heated oil in a frying pan until puffed. Serve immediately.

MAKES 24 TO 30

CHUTNEYS
AND
PICKLES

Chutneys and pickles are best made in large quantities and stored in the fridge in airtight jars, handy to use whenever you need them. The fruit chutneys and pickles are delightfully sweet and spicy, and there are also tangy ones like the tomato pickle.

Serve a selection of these, putting small amounts in little bowls, on the dinner table, or with snacks at a party. Or spread some on a sandwich to liven it up!

Chutneys and pickles are easy to make, involving blending or pounding ingredients together, and then boiling to thicken. Vinegar is an important ingredient, helping to preserve them.

Hot Peach Pickle

SULTANA CHUTNEY

750 g sultanas, roughly chopped

1¾ cups (440 ml) malt vinegar

60 g fresh ginger, thinly sliced

6 garlic cloves, sliced

30 g blanched almonds

2¼ cups (375 g) brown sugar

60 g salt

2 red dried chillies, chopped

1 Soak sultanas in vinegar for 24 hours.

2 Combine sultana mixture in a saucepan with ginger, garlic, almonds, sugar, salt and chillies, bring to the boil, reduce heat to low, simmer uncovered until mixture has reduced and thickened, cool.

3 Pour into sterilised jars, seal well.

MAKES 4 CUPS (1 LITRE)

FRESH MINT CHUTNEY WITH YOGHURT

2 tablespoons desiccated coconut

2 tablespoons hot milk

¼ cup chopped, fresh mint

1 onion, finely chopped

½ green capsicum (pepper), finely chopped

1 cup (250 ml) plain yoghurt

1 Soak coconut in milk for 30 minutes.

2 Add mint, onion, capsicum and yoghurt, stir until combined.

MAKES 2 CUPS (500 ML)

MANGO CHUTNEY

6 medium sized mangoes (green), sliced

1½ (625 ml) malt vinegar

1½ cups (375 g) sugar

4 cloves garlic, crushed

30 g fresh ginger, grated

1 teaspoon chilli powder

60 g slivered almonds

¾ cup (125 g) raisins

1 Combine mangoes in a saucepan with vinegar and sugar, bring to the boil. Reduce heat to low, cover, simmer 5 minutes.

2 Add garlic, ginger and chilli, simmer for 10 minutes. Add the almonds and raisins, simmer for 5 minutes, cool.

3 Pour into sterilised jars, seal well.

MAKES 5 CUPS (1¼ ML)

FRESH RED DATE CHUTNEY

6 dates, seeded

1 small onion, chopped

6 cloves garlic, chopped

½ teaspoon chilli powder

1 teaspoon ground paprika

½ teaspoon ground cumin

2 tablespoons malt vinegar

1 Combine all ingredients in a blender or food processor, blend until smooth.

MAKES ½ CUP (125 ML)

BENGAL APPLE CHUTNEY

8 large cooking apples

1½ cups (250 g) brown sugar

3½ cups (900 ml) malt vinegar

30 g fresh ginger, grated

½ onion, finely chopped

3 cloves garlic, crushed

1½ tablespoons mustard seeds

2 teaspoons salt

2 to 3 teaspoons chilli powder

125 g (¾ cup) raisins

1 Peel and slice apples, combine, in a saucepan, with sugar and vinegar, bring to boil. Cover, reduce heat to low, simmer until apples are tender.

2 Add ginger, onion, garlic, mustard seeds, salt, chilli powder and raisins. Simmer, uncovered, for 15 minutes or until mixture has reduced and thickened, stirring often.

3 When cool, seal in sterilised jars.

MAKES 6 CUPS (1½ LITRES)

CORIANDER CHUTNEY

handful fresh coriander leaves

4 to 6 green chillies, chopped and seeds removed

4 thin slices fresh ginger, chopped

2 cloves garlic, chopped

fresh lemon juice

1 In a mortar and pestle, coriander, chillies, ginger and garlic to a paste.. Add lemon juice to taste.

MAKES ⅓ CUP (80 ML)

COCONUT CHUTNEY

3 tablespoons of desiccated coconut

6 slices fresh ginger, chopped

3 or 4 dry red or fresh chillies, chopped

1 clove garlic, crushed

fresh lemon juice

1 In a mortar and pestle pound coconut, ginger, chilli and garlic with enough lemon juice to mix to a paste.

MAKES ½ CUP (125 ML)

MINT CHUTNEY

heaped teaspoon tamarind (free from stones and fibres), blended to a paste

handful fresh mint leaves

4 to 6 dry or fresh red chillies, chopped

2 cloves garlic, chopped

few drops vinegar

1 In a mortar and pestle pound tamarind, mint, chillies and garlic to a paste. If necessary, add a few drops of vinegar.

MAKES ½ CUP (125 ML)

STEP-BY-STEP TECHNIQUES

HOT PEACH PICKLE

1 kg nearly ripe peaches

3 cups (500 g) brown sugar

1½ (625 ml) white vinegar

250 g seedless sultanas

30 g red chillies, sliced and seeds removed

1 teaspoon ground ginger

1 Blanch peaches in very hot water for 1 minute, remove, peel off skins. Cut peaches in half, remove seeds.

2 Combine sugar and half the vinegar in a saucepan, bring to the boil.

3 Add peaches, reduce heat to low. Cover, simmer until peaches are soft.

4 Add sultanas, chillies, ginger and remaining vinegar. Simmer, uncovered, until mixture has reduced and thickened.

5 When cool, pour into sterilised jars, seal well.

MAKES 4 CUPS (1 LITRE)

Blanch peaches, peel and cut in half or quarters

Cook peaches with sugar and vinegar

Add sultanas, chillies, ginger and vinegar

Hot Peach Pickle

TOMATO PICKLE

3 tomatoes, roughly chopped

4 fresh green chillies, chopped and seeds removed

1 clove garlic, crushed

½ teaspoon sugar

thin slice ginger, chopped

1 small onion, chopped

3 tablespoons white vinegar

1 Blend all ingredients in a food processor, until mixture is smooth.

2 Pour mixture into a saucepan, bring to the boil. Reduce heat to low, simmer until mixture thickens, stirring often.

3 When cool, seal in sterilised jars.

MAKES ½ CUP (125 ML)

GREEN CAPSICUM PICKLE

500 g green capsicums (peppers), sliced

500 g green tomatoes, sliced

8 onions, sliced

½ cup (125 g) salt

3½ cups (600 g) brown sugar

3½ cups (875 ml) white vinegar

2 tablespoons ground cloves

2 tablespoons ground cinnamon

1 Combine capsicums, tomatoes and onions in a bowl, stir in salt. Put a weight on top, stand at least 8 hours, preferably overnight. Remove weight, drain off liquid.

2 Combine vegetables in a saucepan with sugar, vinegar, cloves and cinnamon, bring to the boil, reduce heat to low, cover, simmer for 2 hours, cool.

4 Pour into sterilised jars, seal well.

MAKES 4 CUPS (1 LITRE)

MANGO PICKLE

5 mangoes, roughly chopped

1 cup (230 g) sugar

½ cup (125 ml) white vinegar

5 mm slice fresh ginger, grated

2 teaspoons chilli powder

1 Combine all ingredients, bring to the boil. Reduce heat to low, simmer for 10 minutes or until mangoes are soft and the mixture is jam-like in consistency. Stir often.

2 When cool, seal in sterilised jars.

MAKES 2 CUPS (500 ML)

EGGPLANT PICKLE

2 kg eggplant (aubergine), cut into 2½ cm pieces

125 g green chillies, chopped

2 cloves garlic, crushed

1½ cups (625 ml) white vinegar

2 tablespoons chilli powder

2 teaspoons ground turmeric

2 teaspoons ground ginger

1¼ cups (310 ml) sesame oil

1 tablespoon cumin seeds

1 tablespoon fenugreek seeds

2 heaped tablespoons salt

1 cup (250 g) sugar

30 g fresh ginger, finely chopped

1 Combine garlic with 1 tablespoon vinegar, chilli powder, turmeric and ground ginger, to form a paste.

2 Heat oil to moderate, fry cumin and fenugreek seeds for 1 minute.

3 Add the spice paste, stir over low heat until oil floats on top.

4 Add remaining vinegar, salt, sugar, eggplant, chillies and fresh ginger. Stir over low heat until oil floats on top.

5 When cool, pour into sterilised jars, seal well.

MAKES 5 CUPS (1¼ LITRES)

DESSERTS

While desserts are not the focus of an Indian meal, they are fascinating and very different to the Western idea of dessert. There are amazing combinations of sweet ingredients and aromatic spices, and they often contain nuts such as almonds and pistachios, for additional flavour.

They may be dry cookies or slices and eaten with the fingers, or rich and creamy puddings, eaten in bowls. Whichever one you choose to make, you will not be disappointed with the unusual and exotic taste.

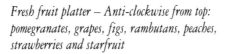

Fresh fruit platter – Anti-clockwise from top: pomegranates, grapes, figs, rambutans, peaches, strawberries and starfruit

BARFI

4 cups (1 litre) milk

¼ cup (60 g) sugar

½ teaspoon cardamom seeds

20 g pistachio nuts

20 g slivered almonds

1 Place milk in a saucepan and bring to the boil. Reduce heat to low, simmer for 40 minutes or until milk has a porridge-like consistency, stirring frequently.

2 Add sugar, stir over heat until dissolved. Add cardamom, pistachios and almonds.

3 Pour into a greased lamington pan and cool. Cut into diamonds to serve.

SERVES 6 TO 8

PASTRY FOR POORIS (PUFFS)

4 cups (500 g) plain flour, sifted

120 g ghee

cold water

extra ghee for frying

1 Place flour in a bowl, rub in ghee. Add enough water to mix to a soft, pliable dough. Knead until smooth.

2 Roll out thinly, cut out circles in the size required.

3 In the centre of each piece, place a quantity of whatever filling you are using, (choose from those below). Wet the edge of the pastry all round with water, fold in half, press the edges down.

4 Melt extra ghee in a frying pan, add pooris 1 to 3 at a time, cook on both sides until golden brown.

MAKES 24

COCONUT FILLING

2⅔ cups (250 g) desiccated coconut, moistened with milk

½ teaspoon ground cardamom

⅓ cup (60 g) sultanas

¼ cup (30 g) ground almonds

½ cup (125 g) of sugar.

1 Blend together all ingredients.

FILLS 36 POORIS

BANANA FILLING

2 ripe bananas, mashed

⅓ cup (30 g) desiccated coconut

sugar

essence of rosewater

1 Mix bananas with the desiccated coconut.

2 Sweeten to taste with sugar and flavour with essence of rosewater.

FILLS 12 POORIS

PINEAPPLE FILLING

340 g can crushed pineapple

½ cup (45 g) desiccated coconut

sugar

1 Drain can of pineapple. Add the desiccated coconut.

2 Sweeten to taste, with sugar.

FILLS 15 POORIS

SEMOLINA COOKIES

2 cups (250 g) plain flour, sifted

¼ cup (45 g) semolina

1 cup (250 g) sugar

¼ teaspoon bicarbonate of soda

150 g ghee, melted

1 In a bowl, mix flour, semolina, sugar and bicarbonate of soda. Add ghee a little at a time, kneading the mixture to a soft dough.

2 Form into balls the size of a large marble,

flatten and place them on baking trays, leaving 4 cm space between them.

3 Bake in moderate oven for about 20 minutes. Cookies will not brown, but should move freely on the tray when cooked.

4 Remove from oven and allow to cool on the trays.

MAKES 40

JALEBI

2 cups (250 g) plain flour, sifted

water

1 tablespoon plain yoghurt

oil for frying

SYRUP

2 cups (500 g) sugar

2½ cups (625 ml) water

¼ teaspoon ground cardamom

pinch of turmeric

1 Place flour into a bowl, make a well in the centre, gradually add water, stirring in gradually increasing circles from the centre. Add sufficient water to form a thin batter. (Alternatively, combine flour and water in a blender or food processor, blend until smooth). Stand 24 hours, stir in yoghurt.

2 Place just sufficient oil in a frying pan to float the jalebis, heat to moderate.

3 Spoon mixture into a piping bag with a 1½ cm plain tube (place a finger over the hole). Pipe the batter in figure eights or double circles into oil, cook on both sides until golden brown. Remove, place into warm syrup for a few minutes. Drain on absorbent paper.

4 TO MAKE SYRUP: Combine all the ingredients in a saucepan, bring to the boil. Simmer over a low heat for 5 to 10 minutes until a thick syrup is formed. Keep warm.

SERVES 4 TO 6

VERMICELLI PUDDING

Coconut-filled Pooris

This is a rich and filling dessert, which can be served hot or cold

2 tablespoons ghee

¼ teaspoon ground cardamom

170 g thin vermicelli

2 cups (500 ml) water

1 cup (230 g) sugar

1 drop yellow food colouring (optional)

60 g blanched almonds, chopped and toasted

125 g cashew nuts, chopped and toasted

30 g shelled pistachio nuts, chopped

2 drops vanilla essence

4 cups (1 litre) milk

1 Melt ghee in a saucepan, sauté cardamom and vermicelli until light brown.

2 Add water and sugar, bring to boil. Reduce heat to moderate, simmer for 10 minutes.

3 Add yellow colouring, almonds, cashews, pistachios, vanilla essence and milk. Bring to the boil and remove from heat, pour into a serving dish.

SERVES 4 TO 6

Steamed Cottage Cheese Sweet and Layered Coconut Milk Cake

STEAMED COTTAGE CHEESE SWEET

500 g cottage cheese

½ cup (125 ml) sweetened condensed milk

4 tablespoons plain yoghurt

2 tablespoons slivered almonds

½ teaspoon ground cardamom

1 Combine cottage cheese with condensed milk and yoghurt, pour into a greased 1 litre ovenproof dish, sprinkle with almonds and cardamom.

4 Place dish into a large baking pan, add enough hot water to come halfway up sides. Cook in a moderate oven for 20 minutes or until mixture has set. Refrigerate until cold, cutting into diamond shapes to serve.

SERVES 4

BANANA FRITTERS

1 cup (125 g) plain flour, sifted

1 egg, beaten

1 small can evaporated milk

4 bananas, halved lengthways

1 cup (250 ml) oil

½ cup (125 g) caster sugar

1 Place flour in a bowl, make a well in the centre of the flour, pour in beaten egg.

2 Blend the egg with the flour a little at a time by stirring in gradually increasing circles from the centre.

3 When almost blended, stir in milk, gradually, to form a smooth batter. Allow to stand for 30 minutes. (Alternatively, combine flour, eggs and milk in blender or food processor, blend until smooth).

4 Heat oil in a frying pan over moderate heat, dip bananas in the batter and deep fry until golden brown. Remove, drain on absorbent paper and roll in caster sugar.

SERVES 4

LAYERED COCONUT MILK CAKE

1⅓ cups (350 g) sugar

½ cup (125 ml) water

1 cup (125 g) plain flour, sifted

2½ cups (625 ml) coconut milk

10 egg yolks, lightly beaten

90 g ghee, melted

1 Combine sugar and water in a saucepan, stir over heat until sugar dissolves, cool.

2 Stir coconut milk into flour, stir in sugar syrup and egg yolks until smooth, stand 1 hour.

3 Preheat grill to moderate, remove grill tray.

4 Pour 2 teaspoons of ghee into an 18 cm round cake pan. Pour in 3 tablespoons of batter, tilt pan until mixture forms a thin layer, grill about 4 minutes or until golden brown.

5 Brush top with melted ghee, pour 3 tablespoons of batter over first layer, grill until golden brown. Repeat until all mixture is finished, brushing each layer with ghee before pouring in the next layer. Lower temperature of grill if necessary. Cake will take approximately 1 hour to cook.

6 Allow cake to cool, turn out, cut into wedges to serve.

SERVES 10

PARSEE CUSTARD

3½ cups (875 ml) milk

¼ cup (60 g) caster sugar

3 eggs

2 egg yolks

1 tablespoon ground almonds

1 tablespoon rose water

pinch ground nutmeg

pinch ground cardamom

1 Combine milk and sugar in a saucepan, simmer over low heat until reduced to half, cool slightly.

2 Lightly beat eggs and egg yolks together, add milk mixture, almonds and rosewater. Stir until combined.

3 Pour into a 1½ litre ovenproof dish, sprinkle with nutmeg and cardamom. Place dish in a pan of hot water, bake in moderate oven for 45 minutes or until custard is set.

SERVES 6 TO 8

❖ **PARSEE CUSTARD**

This custard has a delicate aromatic flavour. It is served at Parsee weddings.

You may like to pour the mixture in small cups or moulds, bake them and serve these individual portions immediately.

SEMOLINA PUDDING

60 g butter

15 g flaked almonds

¾ cup (125 g) semolina

3½ cups (875 ml) milk

½ cup (125 g) caster sugar

1 teaspoon vanilla essence

15 g currants

½ teaspoon ground cardamom

½ teaspoon grated nutmeg

Semolina Pudding

1 Melt butter in a frying pan, sauté almonds until lightly browned, remove from pan, set aside.

2 Add semolina to butter in pan, sauté for 2 minutes.

3 Combine milk and sugar in a saucepan, bring to the boil.

4 Add semolina to milk, stir over heat until mixture has thickened, Stir in vanilla, cool.

5 Spoon into serving dishes, sprinkle with almonds, currants, cardamom and nutmeg.

SERVES 8 TO 10

SWEET SAFFRON RICE

½ teaspoon saffron strands

2 tablespoons hot milk

¾ cup (150 g) rice

45 g ghee

3 cardamom seeds

1 inch stick cinnamon

⅔ cup (170 ml) cold milk

4 tablespoons sugar

2 tablespoons thick cream

30 g flaked almonds, toasted

30 g walnuts (shelled)

¼ cup (30 g) raisins

1 Soak saffron strands in the hot milk.

2 Cook rice in boiling water for 5 minutes, then drain.

3 Melt ghee in a saucepan, sauté rice, cardamom and cinnamon 3 minutes.

4 Add cold milk and sugar, cook over low heat, covered, until the rice is fully cooked.

Add cream and saffron milk, cover, cook for 1 minute.

5 Spoon into serving dish, sprinkle with almonds, walnuts and raisins.

SERVES 6 TO 8

FIRNEE

½ cup (60 g) rice flour

2½ cups (625 ml) milk

⅓ cup (90 g) sugar

1 tablespoon rose water

2 tablespoon slivered almonds

12 shelled pistachio nuts

1 Place rice flour in a saucepan, gradually stir in milk, stir until smooth.

2 Stir constantly over low heat until sauce boils and thickens.

3 Add sugar and rose water, cool.

4 Spoon into serving dishes, top with almonds and pistachios.

SERVES 4 TO 6

❖ **SWEET SAFFRON RICE**

This rich dessert is the Indian equivalent of English creamed rice, with a spicy, aromatic touch

Sweet Saffron Rice

MEASURING MADE EASY

HOW TO MEASURE LIQUIDS

METRIC	IMPERIAL	CUPS
30 ml	1 fluid ounce	1 tablespoon plus 2 teaspoons
60 ml	2 fluid ounces	¼ cup
90 ml	3 fluid ounces	
125 ml	4 fluid ounces	½ cup
150 ml	5 fluid ounces	
170 ml	5 ½ fluid ounces	
180 ml	6 fluid ounces	¾ cup
220 ml	7 fluid ounces	
250 ml	8 fluid ounces	1 cup
500 ml	16 fluid ounces	2 cups
600 ml	20 fluid ounces (1 pint)	2½ cups
1 litre	1¾ pints	

HOW TO MEASURE DRY INGREDIENTS

15 g	½ oz	
30 g	1 oz	
60 g	2 oz	
90 g	3 oz	
125 g	4 oz	(¼ lb)
155 g	5 oz	
185 g	6 oz	
220 g	7 oz	
250 g	8 oz	(½ lb)
280 g	9 oz	
315 g	10 oz	
345 g	11 oz	
375 g	12 oz	(¾ lb)
410 g	13 oz	
440 g	14 oz	
470 g	15 oz	
500 g	16 oz	(1 lb)
750 g	24 oz	(1½ lb)
1 kg	32 oz	(2 lb)

QUICK CONVERSIONS

5 mm	¼ inch	
1 cm	½ inch	
2 cm	¾ inch	
2½ cm	1 inch	
5 cm	2 inches	
6 cm	2½ inches	
8 cm	3 inches	
10 cm	4 inches	
12 cm	5 inches	
15 cm	6 inches	
18 cm	7 inches	
20 cm	8 inches	
23 cm	9 inches	
25 cm	10 inches	
28 cm	11 inches	
30 cm	12 inches	(1 foot)
46 cm	18 inches	
50 cm	20 inches	
61 cm	24 inches	(2 feet)
77 cm	30 inches	

NOTE: We developed the recipes in this book in Australia where the tablespoon measure is 20 ml. In many other countries the tablespoon is 15 ml. For most recipes this difference will not be noticeable.

However, for recipes using baking powder, gelatine, bicarbonate of soda, small amounts of flour and cornflour, we suggest you add an extra teaspoon for each tablespoon specified

USING CUPS AND SPOONS
All cup and spoon measurements are level

METRIC CUP				METRIC SPOONS		
¼ cup	60 ml	2 fluid ounces		¼ teaspoon	1¼ ml	
⅓ cup	80 ml	2½ fluid ounces		½ teaspoon	2½ ml	
½ cup	125 ml	4 fluid ounces		1 teaspoon	5 ml	
1 cup	250 ml	8 fluid ounces		1 tablespoon	20 ml	

OVEN TEMPERATURES

TEMPERATURES	CELSIUS (°C)	FAHRENHEIT (°F)	GAS MARK
Very slow	120	250	½
Slow	150	300	2
Moderately slow	160-180	325-350	3-4
Moderate	190-200	375-400	5-6
Moderately hot	220-230	425-450	7
Hot	250-260	475-500	8-9

INDEX